EDITED BOOK OF
PHARMACEUTICAL INORGANIC CHEMISTRY

EDITOR

Dr. Surya Prakash Gupta

Professor & Director

Rajiv Gandhi Institute of Pharmacy

Faculty of Pharmaceutical Science & Technology

AKS University

Satna (Madhya Pradesh)

EDITOR

Dr. Shailendra Yadav

Associate Professor & Head of Department

Department of Chemistry,

AKS University

Satna (Madhya Pradesh)

EDITOR

Ms. Shikha Singh

Assistant Professor

Rajiv Gandhi Institute of Pharmacy

Faculty of Pharmaceutical Science & Technology

AKS University

Satna (Madhya Pradesh)

Notion Press

EDITED BOOK OF

PHARMACEUTICAL INORGANIC CHEMISTRY

First Edition 2024

Published by:

NOTION PRESS

Publisher and distributor

Head office : Notion press Media Pvt. Ltd.

7,Red cross Road,

Egmore, Chennai,Tamil Nadu 60008

Website: www.notionpress.com

EDITED BOOK OF
PHARMACEUTICAL INORGANIC CHEMISTRY

ABOUT THE EDITORS

Dr. Surya Prakash Gupta is a distinguished academician and currently serves as a Professor and Director at the Rajiv Gandhi Institute of Pharmacy, Constituent Unit of AKS University, Satna (M.P.). With an illustrious career spanning several years, Dr. Gupta has made significant contributions to the field of pharmacy education and research. He holds a Ph.D. in Pharmacy and is widely respected for his expertise in the field. Dr. Gupta's academic journey is marked by numerous achievements, and he has played a pivotal role in shaping the careers of aspiring pharmacists. As the Director of the Rajiv Gandhi Institute of Pharmacy, Dr. Gupta has been instrumental in implementing innovative teaching methodologies and fostering an environment conducive to research and learning. Under his guidance, the institute has achieved new heights of excellence. Dr. Surya Prakash Gupta is not only a proficient academician but also an inspiring mentor who is dedicated to the advancement of pharmacy education in India. His commitment to academic excellence and research makes him a highly regarded figure in the field.

Dr. Shailendra Yadav is an Associate professor & Head of Department in the Department of Chemistry, AKS University Satna, M.P., India. He is also serving as a Director in Centre for Green Chemistry and Sustainability at AKS University, Satna. He obtained Ph.D. in synthetic organic chemistry in 2013 from V.B.S.P.U. Jaunpur, U.P., India. He has published more than 30 research papers in reputed journals and also contributed more than 10 book chapters in books of reputed publishers as well as he has written 1 book and edited 1book. He has published 8 Indian patents of his inventions in which 1 is awarded patent. He is also member of RSC. He has more than 12 years teaching and research experience in research areas of green chemistry, natural products, corrosion science, organic synthesis and environmental chemistry.

 **Ms. Shikha Singh** is currently working as Assistant Professor in Rajiv Gandhi Institute of Pharmacy, AKS University Satna. She has actively participated in academic & research work. She did her M. Pharm in Pharmaceutical Chemistry from premier institute. She has presented paper in various National & International conferences. She is also engaged in various extracurricular activities to the pharmacy profession.

EDITED BOOK
PHARMACEUTICAL INORGANIC CHEMISTRY
NOTION PRESS
PREFACE

The authors feel great pleasure in presenting the **"Edited Book of Pharmaceutical Inorganic Chemistry"** for graduate and post graduate students. The present book on **Edited Book of Pharmaceutical Inorganic Chemistry** has been written according to the syllabus of B. Pharm of Pharmacy Council of India and covers full course of the subject.

THE SALIENT FEATURES OF THE BOOK ARE: -

- *Easy to understand style of writing* which makes the book a self-study material.

- *Each new concept has been introduced through day-today problem of interest* to the students which makes the subject matter interesting.

- *The language of the book, on the whole, is lucid and easy to understand.*

- Wherever needed *neatly labeled figures have been drawn.*

The authors hope that the students, teachers and other readers will find the book interesting and to the point covering the course. We hope that the students will receive the book warmly.

I express a sincere thank you to the Management of Rajiv Gandhi Institute of Pharmacy, Faculty of Pharmaceutical Science & Technology, AKS University for their support during the writing of this book.

Every effort is made to keep the book error free. The author will gratefully acknowledge the suggestions to improve the book to make it more useful. Wishing our readers success in examination and life ahead. The authors feel that their efforts will be fully rewarded if the book serves the purpose for which it is written.

EDITED BOOK OF

PHARMACEUTICAL INORGANIC CHEMISTRY

CONTENTS

S. No.	Particular	Author name, designation, College name and Address	Page number
1.	Impurities in pharmaceutical substances: Sources and types of impurities,	Dr. Surya Prakash Gupta Professor & Director Rajiv Gandhi Institute of Pharmacy Faculty of Pharmaceutical Science & Technology AKS University, Satna (M.P.)	12
2.	History of Pharmacopoeia	Dr. Gopal Garg Professor Rajiv Gandhi Institute of Pharmacy, Faculty of Pharmaceutical Science & Technology, AKS University Satna, MP-India	24
3.	Limit test for chloride and sulphate	Mrs. Kiran Shukla Associate Professor Rajiv Gandhi Institute of Pharmacy, Faculty of Pharmaceutical Science & Technology, AKS University Satna, MP-India	37
4.	Limit test for Iron and Arsenic	Mrs. Shaily Goyal Associate Professor	47

		Rajiv Gandhi Institute of Pharmacy, Faculty of Pharmaceutical Science & Technology, AKS University Satna, MP-India	
5.	Limit test for Heavy metal and lead	Mr. Prabhakar Tiwari Associate Professor Rajiv Gandhi Institute of Pharmacy, Faculty of Pharmaceutical Science & Technology, AKS University Satna, MP-India	56
6.	Acids, Bases and Buffers	Mrs. Priyanka Gupta Associate Professor Rajiv Gandhi Institute of Pharmacy, Faculty of Pharmaceutical Science & Technology, AKS University Satna, MP-India	64
7.	Major extra and intracellular electrolytes	Ms. Neha Goel Associate Professor Rajiv Gandhi Institute of Pharmacy, Faculty of Pharmaceutical Science & Technology, AKS University Satna, MP-India	94
8.	Dental products	Mrs. Priya Diwedi Assistant Professor	119

		Rajiv Gandhi Institute of Pharmacy, Faculty of Pharmaceutical Science & Technology, AKS University Satna, MP-India	
9.	Acidifiers	Mrs. Pooja Chauhan Assistant Professor Rajiv Gandhi Institute of Pharmacy, Faculty of Pharmaceutical Science & Technology, AKS University Satna, MP-India	133
10.	Antacid	Mr. Satyendra Garg Assistant Professor Rajiv Gandhi Institute of Pharmacy, Faculty of Pharmaceutical Science & Technology, AKS University Satna, MP-India	142
11.	Cathartics	Mrs. Neelam Singh Assistant Professor Rajiv Gandhi Institute of Pharmacy, Faculty of Pharmaceutical Science & Technology, AKS University Satna, MP-India	155
12.	Antimicrobials-I	Mr. Abu Tahir Assistant Professor	166

		Rajiv Gandhi Institute of Pharmacy, Faculty of Pharmaceutical Science & Technology, AKS University Satna, MP-India	
13.	Antimicrobials-II	Ms. Shikha Singh Assistant Professor Rajiv Gandhi Institute of Pharmacy, Faculty of Pharmaceutical Science & Technology, AKS University Satna, MP-India	175
14.	Expectorants:	Mrs. Evneet Kaur Bhatia Assistant Professor Rajiv Gandhi Institute of Pharmacy, Faculty of Pharmaceutical Science & Technology, AKS University Satna, MP-India	188
15.	Emetics	Mrs. Neha Soni Assistant Professor Rajiv Gandhi Institute of Pharmacy, Faculty of Pharmaceutical Science & Technology, AKS University Satna, MP-India	197
16.	Haematinics	Mrs. Priyanka Soni Assistant Professor	203

		Rajiv Gandhi Institute of Pharmacy, Faculty of Pharmaceutical Science & Technology, AKS University Satna, MP-India	
17.	Poison and Antidote	Mr. Prabhanshu Vaishya Assistant Professor Rajiv Gandhi Institute of Pharmacy, Faculty of Pharmaceutical Science & Technology, AKS University Satna, MP-India	210
18.	Astringents	Mr. Santosh Kumar Assistant Professor Rajiv Gandhi Institute of Pharmacy, Faculty of Pharmaceutical Science & Technology, AKS University Satna, MP-India	218
19.	Radiopharmaceuticals-I	Mr. Ram Prasad Sahu Assistant Professor Rajiv Gandhi Institute of Pharmacy, Faculty of Pharmaceutical Science & Technology, AKS University Satna, MP-India	224
20.	Radiopharmaceuticals-II	Mr. Sachin Singh Assistant Professor	235

		Rajiv Gandhi Institute of Pharmacy, Faculty of Pharmaceutical Science & Technology, AKS University Satna, MP-India	

CHAPTER – 1

IMPURITIES IN PHARMACEUTICAL SUBSTANCES

Dr. Surya Prakash Gupta

Professor & Director, Rajiv Gandhi Institute of Pharmacy, Faculty of Pharmaceutical Science & Technology, AKS University, Satna (M.P.)

ABSTRACT:

Impurities in pharmaceutical substances are a critical concern in drug development and manufacturing, as they can significantly impact the safety, efficacy, and quality of medications. These impurities can arise from various sources, including raw materials, synthesis processes, degradation, and contamination during manufacturing or storage. Types of impurities commonly encountered include organic impurities, inorganic impurities, and residual solvents. Organic impurities may result from starting materials, intermediates, or by-products formed during synthesis. Inorganic impurities often originate from reagents, catalysts, or other inorganic materials used in the manufacturing process. Residual solvents are organic volatile chemicals used in the production process that must be removed to acceptable levels. The presence of these impurities is closely monitored through rigorous testing and quality control measures, following guidelines set by regulatory bodies such as the International Council for Harmonisation (ICH). Identifying and quantifying impurities is essential to ensure that pharmaceutical products meet safety standards and therapeutic requirements. Advanced analytical techniques like high-performance liquid chromatography (HPLC), gas chromatography (GC), and mass spectrometry (MS) are employed to detect and characterize impurities. The acceptable limits of impurities are defined based on their potential toxicity and the maximum daily dose of the drug. Effective impurity control strategies are vital to minimize risks and ensure the production of high-quality pharmaceutical products.

Definition: A compound is said to be impure if it is having foreign matter, i.e. impurities.

Chemical purity implies freedom from foreign matter. It means that a pure chemical refers to that compound which is having no foreign matter, i.e. impurities.

Types of Impurities:

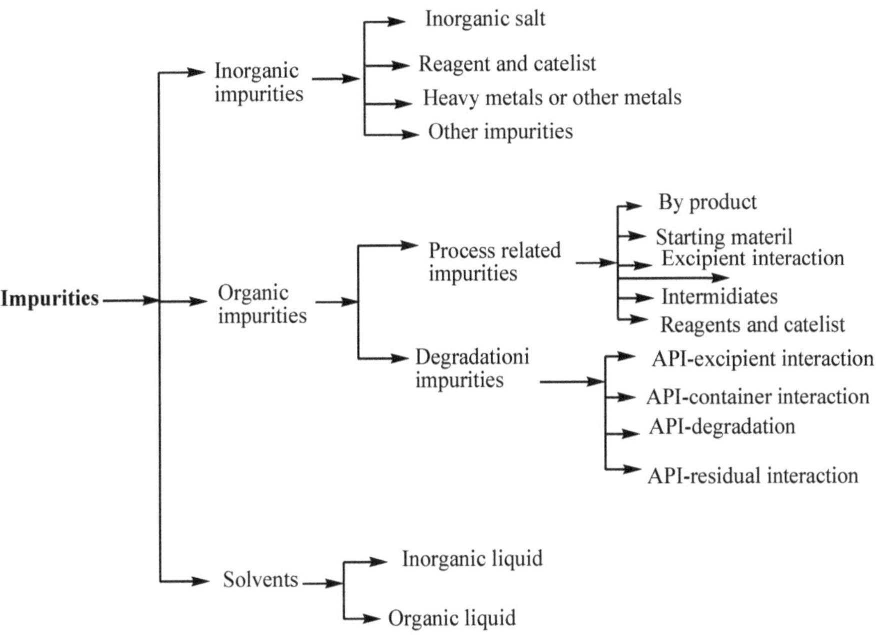

API- Active Pharmaceutical Ingredients

TYPE OF IMPURITIES

Impure Pharmaceutical substance: Any pharmaceutical substance is said to be impure, if it is having foreign matter.

Pure Pharmaceutical substance: Any pharmaceutical substance is said to be pure, if it is completely free from any kind of foreign matter.

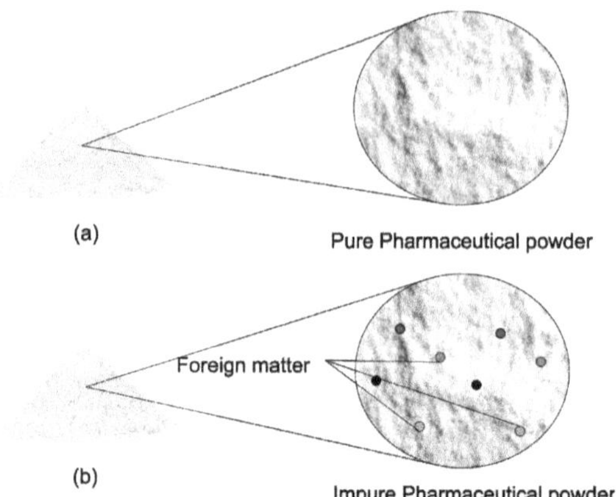

Fig. 1. Difference between pure and impure pharmaceutical powder

Types of Impurities

1. Organic Impurities:

    a. Starting Materials: Unreacted raw materials used in the synthesis of the active pharmaceutical ingredient (API).

    b. Intermediates: Compounds formed during the synthesis of the API that are not fully converted to the final product.

    c. By-products: Unintended compounds formed as side reactions during the synthesis process.

    d. Degradation Products: Compounds formed by the chemical breakdown of the API or excipients over time.

    e. Residual Solvents: Organic solvents used in the manufacturing process that are not completely removed.

2. Inorganic Impurities:

    a. Reagents and Ligands: Inorganic chemicals used during the synthesis that may remain in trace amounts.

    b. Catalysts: Metal catalysts used in chemical reactions, such as palladium, platinum, or copper, that can remain as residues.

    c. Heavy Metals: Trace amounts of toxic metals such as lead, mercury, arsenic, and cadmium, which can come from raw materials or manufacturing equipment.

    d. Inorganic Salts: Salts used in the synthesis or purification processes, such as sodium chloride or potassium bromide.

3. Residual Solvents:

    a. Class 1 Solvents: Solvents to be avoided due to their toxicity, such as benzene and carbon tetrachloride.

    b. Class 2 Solvents: Solvents to be limited due to their potential toxicity, such as methanol, toluene, and acetonitrile.

    c. Class 3 Solvents: Solvents with low toxic potential, such as ethanol and acetone, which should be controlled.

4. Elemental Impurities:

    a. Class 1 Elements: Elements like arsenic, cadmium, mercury, and lead, which have significant toxicity.

    b. Class 2A and 2B Elements: Elements like cobalt, nickel, and vanadium (2A) and thallium, gold, and silver (2B), which have moderate toxicity.

    c. Class 3 Elements: Elements with relatively low toxicity, such as iron, zinc, and copper.

5. Microbial Impurities:

    a. Bacterial Contaminants: Pathogenic or non-pathogenic bacteria that can affect product safety.

    b. Fungal Contaminants: Molds and yeasts that can grow in or on the product.

    c. Endotoxins: Toxic components from bacterial cell walls, particularly from Gram-negative bacteria, that can cause severe reactions.

6. Physical Impurities:

a. Particulate Matter: Foreign particles such as dust, fibers, and other extraneous contaminants.

b. Glass, Metal, and Plastic Fragments: Contaminants from manufacturing equipment or packaging materials.

7. Environmental Impurities:

a. Airborne Contaminants: Dust, pollen, and other airborne particles from the manufacturing environment.

b. Waterborne Contaminants: Impurities present in water used during the manufacturing process, such as dissolved minerals and organic matter.

8. Packaging Material Leachables:

a. Plasticizers: Chemicals used in plastic packaging that can leach into the pharmaceutical product.

b. Stabilizers: Compounds added to packaging materials to maintain their integrity, which can contaminate the product.

c. Residual Monomers: Unreacted monomers from polymer packaging materials that can leach into the product.

SOURCE OF IMPURITIES:

1) Raw Materials and Starting Materials:

a) Impurities in Raw Materials: Contaminants present in the raw materials used to synthesize the active pharmaceutical ingredient (API).

b) Starting Materials: Unreacted starting materials that remain in the final product if the reaction is incomplete.

2) Reagents, Solvents, and Catalysts:

a) Reagents: Chemical reagents used in the synthesis process can introduce impurities if not completely removed.

b) Solvents: Residual solvents from the manufacturing process that are not fully evaporated or removed during purification.

c) Catalysts: Metal catalysts used in chemical reactions that can remain as residues in the final product.

d) Solvents:

Water is the cheapest solvent and is commonly used especially in the manufacture of inorganic chemicals.

- Tap water contains sodium, magnesium, chlorides, sulphates and carbonates as impurities though in very small amounts.

- Softened water is prepared by passing tap water through sodium form of zeolite which removes the divalent cation from tap water in exchange for sodium. In other words, soft water is free from calcium and magnesium salts but contains more quantities of sodium salt.

- De-mineralized water is prepared by passing tap water columns containing ion-exchange resins, and is free from calcium, magnesium, sodium, chlorides, sulphates, carbonates, etc. It may although contain organic impurities.

- Distilled water is free from all organic and inorganic impurities and is, therefore, the best as solvent. But it is quite costly.

3) Reaction By-products:

a) Side Reactions: Unintended chemical reactions that produce by-products, which can contaminate the final product.

b) Decomposition Products: Degradation of reagents, solvents, or intermediates during the synthesis process.

4) Synthesis Process:

a) Incomplete Reactions: When reactions do not go to completion, leaving unreacted starting materials and intermediates.

b) Process Conditions: Variations in temperature, pH, or other reaction conditions that can lead to the formation of impurities.

5) Purification Process:

a) Inadequate Purification: Insufficient purification steps that fail to remove all impurities from the final product.

b) Adsorbents and Filter Media: Residues from purification agents or materials used in filtration and separation processes.

6) Degradation:

a) Chemical Degradation: Breakdown of the API or excipients over time due to exposure to light, heat, moisture, or reactive chemicals.

b) Physical Degradation: Physical changes such as polymorphic transformations, crystallization, or aggregation that can affect the purity of the substance.

7) Environmental Contaminants:

a) Airborne Particles: Dust, pollen, and other particulate matter from the manufacturing environment.

b) Water Contaminants: Impurities present in water used during the synthesis or purification processes, such as dissolved minerals and organic matter.

8) Packaging and Storage:

a) Leachables: Chemicals that leach from packaging materials into the pharmaceutical product.

b) Adsorption: Active ingredients or excipients adsorbing onto the surface of packaging materials.

c) Storage Conditions: Environmental factors like temperature, humidity, and light that can cause degradation of the product during storage.

9) Microbial Contaminants:

a) Microbial Contamination: Introduction of bacteria, fungi, or other microorganisms during the manufacturing process.

b) Endotoxins: Toxins released from bacterial cells that can contaminate the product.

10) Atmospheric contamination during the manufacturing process:

- Industrial area contains dust particles (aluminium oxide, silica glass particles, plastic fragments, etc) and some gases such as sulphur dioxide H2S and black smoke
- Example: Sodium hydroxide readily absorb carbon dioxide

$$NaOH + CO_2 \quad = \quad Na_2CO_3 + H_2O$$

11) Manufacturing Equipment:
   a) Equipment Wear and Tear: Metal shavings, plastic fragments, or other contaminants from the wear and tear of manufacturing equipment.
   b) Cleaning Agents: Residues from cleaning agents used to sanitize manufacturing equipment and facilities.

12) Handling and Processing:
   a) Cross-contamination: Contamination from other products or substances handled in the same facility.
   b) Operator Handling: Introduction of impurities from personnel handling the product during manufacturing and packaging.

EFFECTS OF IMPURITIES:

Impurities in pharmaceutical inorganic substances can have specific effects on the safety, efficacy, and quality of the drug product. Here are the key effects of impurities in pharmaceutical inorganic substances:

1) Safety:
   a) Toxicity: Inorganic impurities, such as heavy metals (lead, mercury, arsenic, cadmium), can be highly toxic even at trace levels, leading to acute or chronic toxicity.
   b) Allergic Reactions: Certain inorganic impurities can cause allergic reactions in sensitive individuals.
   c) Carcinogenicity: Some inorganic impurities, like certain heavy metals, are known carcinogens and can increase the risk of cancer.

d) Mutagenicity: Inorganic impurities may cause genetic mutations, potentially leading to birth defects or other genetic disorders.

e) Endotoxins: Although typically associated with biological contaminants, certain inorganic impurities can exacerbate immune responses.

2) Efficacy:

a) Reduced Potency: Inorganic impurities can reduce the concentration of the active pharmaceutical ingredient (API), leading to a decrease in the drug's potency and therapeutic effectiveness.

b) Interference with API: Inorganic impurities can chemically interact with the API, potentially altering its pharmacokinetic and pharmacodynamic properties, which can reduce efficacy.

c) Stability: Inorganic impurities can catalyze degradation reactions, affecting the stability and shelf-life of the API.

3) Quality:

a) Physical Appearance: Inorganic impurities can alter the color, clarity, and overall appearance of the drug product, making it unacceptable to patients and healthcare providers.

b) Solubility and Dissolution: Inorganic impurities can affect the solubility and dissolution rate of the API, impacting bioavailability and therapeutic effect.

c) Formulation Issues: Inorganic impurities can interfere with the manufacturing process, leading to problems in the formulation of drug delivery systems (e.g., tablets, capsules, injectables).

d) Crystallization: Certain inorganic impurities can affect the crystallization process of APIs, potentially leading to polymorphic forms with different solubility and bioavailability.

4) Regulatory Compliance:

a) Non-compliance: Exceeding acceptable limits of inorganic impurities can result in non-compliance with regulatory standards, leading to product recalls, fines, or other legal consequences.

b) Market Approval: The presence of inorganic impurities above regulatory thresholds can prevent the approval of new drug products or lead to the suspension of existing product approvals.

5) Patient Perception:

a) Trust and Acceptance: Impurities affecting the physical appearance or causing adverse reactions can erode patient trust and acceptance of the drug product.

b) Therapeutic Outcome: Patients may not achieve the desired therapeutic outcome due to reduced efficacy or increased side effects caused by inorganic impurities.

6) Economic Impact:

a) Cost of Recalls: The presence of inorganic impurities can lead to costly product recalls, impacting the financial health of pharmaceutical companies.

b) Additional Testing and Purification: Ensuring control of inorganic impurities often requires additional testing, purification steps, and quality assurance measures, increasing manufacturing costs.

ANALYTICAL QUALITY CONTROL OF FINISHED/ FINAL PRODUCT:

1. Description: Colour, odour, taste, and crystalline form
2. Solubility
3. Identification: Physiochemical and spectroscopically
4. Test for purity

   - Colour, odour and test
   - Physicochemical constant

- Acidity, alkalinity and pH

- Anion and cation

- Moisture determination

- Insoluble residue

- Loss of drying/ ignition

- Ash, sulphated ash and water insoluble ash

- Organic impurities and readily carbonisable substances

- Other physiochemical parameters: Sedimentation volume, bulkiness,

5. Assay:

- Redox titration

- Acid base titration

- gravimetrically

- Non-aqueous titration

- Complexometric titration

SOURCES TO CONTROL IMPURITIES

1. **Washing:** When water soluble substance has to be washed away and water insoluble substances is needed. Chalk from native C_aCO_3, water soluble substances are washed with water and dried and is required to have NLT 97% C_aCO_3 on dry basis while precipitate C_aCO_3 as water insoluble subs. is required to have NLT 98.5% of C_aCO_3 after drying in a manner which is similar to that used for prepared chalk.

2. **Drying:** Generally dried in air Anhydrous chemicals—Vacuum drying has been an impurified unit operation and needs care and precaution so that chemicals may not deteriorate due to oxidation, caking or mould growth.

3. **Re-crystallization of solid substances from water**

Re-crystallization is most common method of purifying soluble salts. With a few exceptions, the solubility of salt in a solvent get increase with increase in temperature and hence a saturated. Solution is allowed to cool slowly after which crystals of a greater purity could be obtained. Sublimation: Applicable to very few substances e.g., AS_2O_3, I, $HgCl_2$, sublimed sulphur. The organic compounds purified by this process are camphor and benzoic acid.

CHAPTER – 2

HISTORY OF PHARMACOPOEIA

Dr. Gopal Garg

Professor, Rajiv Gandhi Institute of Pharmacy, Faculty of Pharmaceutical Science & Technology, AKS University, Satna (M.P.)

ABSTRACT:

The term "pharmacopoeia" comes from the ancient Greek words "pharmakon" (meaning drug) and "poiein" (meaning to make). A pharmacopoeia is a legal and official book issued by recognized authorities, usually appointed by the government, which sets standards and quality indices for drugs, raw materials, and pharmaceutical products. It contains directions for identifying samples and preparing compound medicines, with individual drug or product descriptions called monographs.

Importance of Pharmacopoeia

1. Ensures uniform standards and controls adulterated medicines
2. Essential for medicines licensing and inspection processes
3. Plays a significant role in generic drug manufacturing, contract research, and export production
4. Updated regularly through addenda or new editions to include new drugs and remove outdated ones

Examples of Pharmacopoeias

Many Countries own pharmacopoeia:

Name of country	Name of Pharmacopoeia	Acronym
India	Indian Pharmacopoeia	IP

United States Of America	United States Pharmacopoeia	USP
United Kingdom	British Pharmacopoeia	BP
European Countries	European Pharmacopoeia (Pharmacopoeia Europaea)	Ph.Eur.
Japan	Japanese Pharmacopoeia	JP
China	Pharmacopoeia Of The Peoples's Republic	PPRC
Globally	International Pharmacopoeia (Pharmacopoeia Internationalis)	Ph.Int.

Ancient Precursors to Modern Pharmacopoeia

1. Edwin Smith Papyrus (1862): Oldest surgical treatise
2. De Materia Medica (79 A.D.): Written by Roman physician Dioscorides
3. The Canon of Medicine (1025): Compiled by Persian philosopher Ibn Sina (Avicenna)
4. Shen Nong's Materia Medica: Earliest Chinese pharmacopoeia

Types of Drug Compendia

1. Official Compendia: Legal standards of purity, quality, and strength recognized by government agencies.
   - Examples: British Pharmacopoeia, Indian Pharmacopoeia, United States Pharmacopoeia
2. Non-Official Compendia: Secondary reference sources for drugs and related substances.

- Examples: Merck Index, Extra Pharmacopoeia (Martindale), The United States Dispensatory

INDIAN PHARMACOPOEIA

Under the Drugs and Cosmetics Act 1940 , The Indian Pharmacopoeia is an official book that contains the standards for drugs and other related substances included in the pharmacopoeia. The drugs and other related substances prepared by pharmaceutical manufacturers must comply with these standards . For the preparation of Pharmacopoeia of India, the pharmacopoeias of other countries, like British, Europe, United States, USSR, Japan, the National Formulary (USA) and Merck Index were consulted.

History of Indian Pharmacopoeia:

- The process of publishing the first Pharmacopoeia started in the year 1944 under the chairmanship of Col. R. N. Chopra
- In 1948 government of India appointed an Indian Pharmacopeia committee for preparing 'Pharmacopeia of India'.
- 1st edition I. P. 1955 was published in the official gazette. Dr. B. N. Ghosh, Chairman
    - Supplement 1960

- 2nd edition I. P. 1966, Dr. B. Mukherji, Chairman, Shankar S.

    - Supplement 1975

- 3rd edition I. P. 1985, Dr. Nityanand, Chairman

    - I Addendum/Supplement 1989
    - II Addendum/Supplement 1991
- 4th edition I. P. 1996 Dr. Nityanand, Chairman
    - III Addendum/ Supplement 2000
    - IV Addendum/ Supplement 2002
- 5th edition I. P., 2007, Dr. Nityanand, Chairman

- 6th edition I. P., 2010
- 7th edition I. P. 2014V Addendum/Supplement 2015
- 8th edition IP 2018 (The Indian Pharmacopoeia Commission (IPC) has released the Eighth Edition of Indian Pharmacopoeia (IP-2018). It was released by the Secretary, Ministry of Health & Family Welfare, Government of India)

Contents of the IP 2014 Volume-1:

1. Introduction General Chapters
2. General Notices
3. Test Methods
4. Apparatus
5. Biological Methods
6. Chemical Methods
7. Physical and Physicochemical Methods
8. Pharmaceutical Methods
9. Tests on Herbal Products
10. Tests on Vaccines
11. Tests on Blood and Blood Blood-related Products
12. Reference Data
13. Reagents and Solutions
14. General Tests
15. Containers
16. Tables

Contents of the IP 2014 Volume-2:

1. General Notices General Monographs on Dosage Forms Monographs on Drug substances, Dosage forms and Pharmaceutical Aids
2. Monographs A to M

Contents of the IP 2014 Volume-3:

1. General Notices

2. Monographs on Drug substances,

3. Dosage forms and Pharmaceutical aids

4. Monographs N to Z

5. Monographs on Vaccines and Immunosera for Human Use

6. Monographs on Herbs and Herbal Products

7. Monographs on Blood and Blood Blood related Products

8. Monographs on Biotechnology Products

Contents of the IP 2014 Volume-4:

1. Monographs on Veterinary Products o

2. Non Non-Biological

3. Biological

4. Diagnostics Index

MONOGRAPH:

1. Title of the Monograph: The main name of the substance (The International Non-proprietary Name (INN) approved by the World Health Organization (WHO)).

2. Subsidiary or abbreviated title or synonym : The common name(s), if any, of the substance.

3. Chemical formula and Molecular Weight of the substance : If necessary, its I.U.P.A.C. chemical name and/or its chemical structure is also given .

4. Standards: Prescribes the standards of purity and strength e.g. Sodium bicarbonate IP contains not less than 99.0 % and not more than 100.5 % of NaHCO3.

5. Description: A brief description of the physical form of the material, including colour, texture, whether hygroscopic, odour, if readily apparent, and any other characteristic.

6. Solubility :

7. Identification: At least two or three identification tests, starting with physical and instrumental tests and ending with general chemical reactions is given.

8. Tests of purity: These tests include melting point, boiling point, weight per ml, limit tests for chloride, sulfates, iron, heavy metals, lead and arsenic, specific optical rotation, sulfated ash, loss on drying, pH of solution, etc. as may be applicable for the substance.

9. Method of Assay: The term 'Assay' is used in pharmacopoeias for quantitative determination of principal ingredients of the official substances and of their preparations.

10. Storage: Prescribes some conditions for the storage of some official substances which are likely to deteriorate if not properly stored.

Other Notable Pharmacopoeias

British Pharmacopoeia (BP)

The British Pharmacopoeia (BP) is an authoritative collection of standards for UK medicinal products and pharmaceutical substances. First published in 1864, the BP ensures the quality and safety of medicines by setting out legally binding standards.

History

    a. 1864: First edition published.

    b. 1948: Seventh edition, after which new editions were published at intervals of five years (1948, 1953, 1958, 1963, 1968, 1973).

    c. 1980 & 1988: Subsequent editions.

    d. 1993 onwards: New editions published every year.

Structure

The BP contains:

1. Monographs: Detailed standards for active substances, excipients, and formulated preparations.
2. General Notices: Information and instructions applicable to all monographs.
3. Appendices: Methods of analysis, reagents, and reference spectra.
4. Addendums: Published periodically to update the BP between main editions.

Key Features

a. Monographs: Define the quality standards for individual medicines, including tests and assay methods.
b. General Notices: Provide instructions on interpretation and application of the standards.
c. Appendices: Include methods for physical, chemical, and biological testing.
d. Reference Spectra: Offer standard spectral data for substances to ensure consistency.

Importance

o Quality Assurance: Ensures medicines meet the required standards of quality, safety, and efficacy.
o Legal Standards: Provides legally enforceable specifications for medicinal products.
o International Trade: Facilitates the export and import of pharmaceutical products by providing recognized standards.
o Regulatory Compliance: Assists in the licensing, inspection, and regulation of medicines.

British Pharmaceutical Codex

The British Pharmaceutical Codex (BPC) is related to the BP but includes additional information and standards:

a. More Comprehensive: Contains more drugs and preparations than the BP.

b. Standards for Non-BP Drugs: Provides standards for drugs and preparations not included in the BP.

c. Usage Information: Includes information on drug actions, uses, side effects, precautions, and treatment of poisoning.

d. Preparation Details: Offers formulas, preparation methods, dosage, container, and storage conditions for various pharmaceutical forms.

United States Pharmacopoeia-National Formulary (USP-NF)

The United States Pharmacopoeia-National Formulary (USP-NF) is an official compendium of standards for drugs, dietary supplements, and other healthcare products in the United States. It plays a critical role in ensuring the quality, safety, and efficacy of these products.

History

a. 1820: The first United States Pharmacopoeia (USP) was published by the United States Pharmacopoeial Convention.

b. 1888: The National Formulary (NF) was first published under the guidance of the American Pharmaceutical Association.

c. 1974: The United States Pharmacopoeial Convention acquired the National Formulary.

d. 1980 onwards: The USP and NF were combined into a single publication known as the USP-NF.

Structure

The USP-NF is divided into two main parts:

1. United States Pharmacopoeia (USP): Contains monographs for drug substances, dosage forms, and compounded preparations.
2. National Formulary (NF): Contains monographs for excipients, dietary supplements, and other health care products.

Key Features

    a. Monographs: Detailed standards for identity, strength, quality, and purity of substances. They include specifications for ingredients, preparation methods, and tests.

    b. General Chapters: Provide methods for tests, assays, and procedures that apply to multiple monographs.

    c. General Notices: Guidelines for interpreting and applying the standards throughout the USP-NF.

    d. Reagents and Solutions: Specifications for chemicals and solutions used in tests and assays.

Importance

    a. Quality Assurance: Ensures that products meet high standards of quality and purity.

    b. Legal Standards: Recognized by the Federal Food, Drug, and Cosmetic Act, making it enforceable by law for drugs marketed in the United States.

    c. Regulatory Compliance: Helps manufacturers comply with FDA regulations for drug approval and quality control.

    d. International Trade: Facilitates global commerce by providing recognized standards that enhance product consistency and reliability.

Applications

a. Pharmaceutical Industry: Used by manufacturers to ensure product quality during development, production, and quality control.

b. Healthcare Professionals: Provides a reference for pharmacists, doctors, and other healthcare providers to verify the quality and proper use of medicines.

c. Regulatory Authorities: Utilized by the FDA and other regulatory bodies to enforce drug quality standards and approve new products.

d. Education and Research: A valuable resource for educational institutions and researchers in the fields of pharmacy, medicine, and healthcare.

Extra Pharmacopoeia (Martindale:

The Extra Pharmacopoeia, commonly known as Martindale, is a renowned reference work in the field of pharmaceuticals and medicine. It serves as an extensive encyclopedia of drugs and related substances, providing comprehensive information on their properties, uses, and standards.

History

a. 1883: First produced by William Martindale.

b. Publisher: Published by The Royal Pharmaceutical Society of Great Britain.

c. Purpose: Originally aimed to describe drugs outside the scope of the British Pharmacopoeia.

Scope and Content

a. Comprehensive Coverage: Includes drugs in clinical use worldwide, investigational and veterinary drugs, herbal and complementary medicines, pharmaceutical excipients, vitamins, nutritional agents, vaccines, radiopharmaceuticals, contrast media, diagnostic agents, medicinal gases, drugs of abuse, recreational drugs, toxic substances, disinfectants, and pesticides.

b. Detailed Information: Provides extensive details on each substance, including chemical structures, physical properties, pharmacological effects, therapeutic uses, dosage forms, and storage conditions.

c. Reference Tool: Widely used by healthcare professionals, researchers, and regulatory authorities for reliable and authoritative information.

Key Features

a. Global Perspective: Covers drugs and substances from various international sources, making it valuable for global pharmaceutical practices.

b. Complementary to Pharmacopoeias: Supplements official pharmacopoeias by including additional substances and detailed therapeutic information.

c. Updates: Regularly updated to reflect new developments, emerging substances, and changes in medical practices.

Importance

a. Information Resource: Provides essential data for prescribing medications, formulating treatments, and conducting research in pharmaceutical sciences.

b. Clinical Application: Helps healthcare professionals make informed decisions about drug selection, dosage, and administration.

c. Regulatory Use: Used by regulatory agencies for evaluating drug safety, efficacy, and quality standards.

d. Educational Tool: Valuable for training pharmacists, physicians, and pharmaceutical scientists in understanding drug properties and uses.

MERCK INDEX

The Merck Index is a renowned reference work and authoritative source of information on chemicals, drugs, and biologicals. It serves as an essential tool for scientists, researchers, pharmacists, and professionals seeking detailed and reliable data on substances used in various scientific and industrial fields.

History

a. First Edition: Published in 1889 by Merck & Co., Inc., Rahway, New Jersey, USA.

b. Editions: Continuously updated with new editions to reflect advancements in scientific knowledge and changes in substance properties and uses.

c. Publisher: Originally published by Merck & Co., Inc., it remains a standard reference work in the field of chemistry and pharmaceuticals.

Scope and Content

a. Comprehensive Coverage: Includes detailed information on chemicals, drugs, and biological substances, their properties, uses, synthesis, structure, physical constants, and safety data.

b. Global Relevance: Covers substances used worldwide in various industries, including pharmaceuticals, chemicals, biotechnology, and research.

c. Authoritative Information: Provides verified and up-to-date data compiled by experts in chemistry, pharmacology, and related fields.

Key Features

a. Chemical and Drug Information: Offers comprehensive details on chemical structures, molecular formulas, physical properties (e.g., melting point, boiling point), spectral data (e.g., NMR, IR), and biological activity.

b. Synthesis and Production: Includes methods of synthesis, purification, and production of substances.

c. Safety and Toxicity: Provides information on safety precautions, hazards, toxicity levels, and handling guidelines.

d. References and Citations: Includes references to scientific literature and citations for further reading and verification.

Importance

a. Scientific Research: Used extensively in academic research, pharmaceutical development, chemical synthesis, and industrial applications.

b. Quality Control: Aids in quality control and assurance by providing standards for purity, identification, and characterization of substances.

c. Drug Discovery and Development: Facilitates drug discovery efforts by offering comprehensive data on pharmacological properties and biological activity.

d. Educational Tool: Valuable resource for education and training in chemistry, pharmacology, toxicology, and related scientific disciplines.

CHAPTER – 3

LIMIT TESTS FOR CHLORIDE AND SULPHATE

Mrs. Kiran Shukla

Associate Professor, Rajiv Gandhi Institute of Pharmacy, Faculty of Pharmaceutical Science & Technology, AKS University Satna, MP-India

----

ABSTRACT:

Limit tests are essential analytical procedures in pharmaceutical and chemical industries to determine whether specific impurities in a substance are within acceptable limits. These tests are designed to ensure that impurities, which could affect the safety, efficacy, or stability of the product, do not exceed prescribed levels. The tests involve comparing the intensity of a reaction (often a color change or precipitation) between the test substance and a standard solution containing a known amount of the impurity. Common limit tests include those for heavy metals, chlorides, sulfates, iron, and specific elements like lead and arsenic. These tests are performed using standardized methods outlined in pharmacopeia's such as the USP (United States Pharmacopeia) or EP (European Pharmacopeia). The principle behind these tests is based on visual or instrumental comparison, ensuring that the observed reaction does not exceed the response of the standard. Limit tests are crucial for quality control and regulatory compliance, ensuring that products are safe for consumer use. They provide a quick and cost-effective means to screen for potentially harmful contaminants in raw materials, intermediates, and finished products. By adhering to stringent limit test protocols, manufacturers can uphold the integrity and quality of their pharmaceutical substances, thereby protecting public health.

DEFINITIUON:

Limit tests are quantitative or semi quantitative test designed to identify and control small quantities of impurities which are likely to be present in the substances.

- Tests being used to identify the impurity.
- Tests being used to control the impurity.

GENERAL PRINCIPLE

- If the sample is lighter than the standard solution then it is within the pharmacopeial limit (accepted)
- If the sample is darker/heavier than the standard solution then it is above the pharmacopeial limit (rejected)

GENERAL PRECAUTION

- The liquid used must be clean and filtered if necessary
- The Nessler cylinder must be made of colorless glass and of the same inner diameter
- Detecting opalescence or color development must be performed in daylight
- When comparing turbidity it should be done against black background
- When comparing color it should be done against white background

LIMIT TEST FOR CHLORIDE

The limit test for chloride is a quality control procedure used to ensure that the chloride content in pharmaceutical substances does not exceed specified limits. Chlorides can be present as impurities in raw materials, intermediates, or finished products, potentially affecting the safety and efficacy of pharmaceuticals. This test is essential for maintaining product quality and regulatory compliance. It involves a precipitation reaction where chloride ions react with silver nitrate to form an insoluble silver chloride precipitate, which can be compared visually or instrumentally with a standard.

Principle:

Limit test of chloride is based on the reaction between silver nitrate and soluble chloride to obtain silver chloride which is insoluble in dilute nitric acid.

$$NaCl + AgNO_3 \xrightarrow{HNO_3} AgCl + NaNO_3$$

The silver chloride produced in the presence of dilute nitric acid makes the solution turbid, the extent of turbidity depends upon the amount of chloride present in the substance is compared with a standard opalescence produced by addition of silver nitrate to a standard solution having a known amount of chloride and the same amount of dilute nitric acid as used in the test solution.

Procedure:

S. No	Test	Standard
1.	Dissolve specific quantity of sample in distilled water and transfer in Nessler cylinder	Take 1 ml of 0.05845% w/v solution of sodium chloride (NaCl)
2.	Add 1 ml of nitric acid	Add 1 ml of nitric acid
3.	Dilute to 50 ml with distilled water.	Dilute to 50 ml with distilled water.
4.	Add 1 ml of silver nitrate solution (5%).	Add 1 ml of silver nitrate solution.
5.	Keep a side for 5 minutes	Keep a side for 5 minutes
6.	Observe for opalescence	Observe for opalescence

Observation: The opalescence produce in sample solution should not be greater than standard solution. If opalescence produces in sample solution is less than the standard solution, the sample will pass the limit test of chloride and visa versa.

Reasoning:

Nitric acid is added in the limit test of chloride to make solution acidic and helps silver chloride precipitate to make solution **turbid** at the end of process.

Questions and Answers on Limit Test for Chloride

1. **What is the purpose of the limit test for chloride in pharmaceuticals?**

    - The limit test for chloride ensures that the chloride content in pharmaceutical substances does not exceed specified limits to maintain product safety and quality.

2. **What principle is the limit test for chloride based on?**

    - The principle is based on the formation of an insoluble silver chloride precipitate when silver nitrate reacts with chloride ions in the sample.

3. **Which reagent is added to the sample to detect chloride ions?**

    - Silver nitrate ($AgNO_3$) is added to the sample to react with chloride ions and form silver chloride ($AgCl$) precipitate.

4. **Why is dilute nitric acid added to the sample solution before the silver nitrate?**

    - Dilute nitric acid is added to prevent the precipitation of other silver salts and to ensure the reaction is specific to chloride ions.

5. **How is the intensity of the precipitate compared in the limit test for chloride?**

    - The intensity of the precipitate is compared visually or using instruments like a nephelometer or turbidimeter against a standard chloride solution.

6. **What forms the white precipitate in the limit test for chloride?**

    - The white precipitate is silver chloride ($AgCl$), which forms when chloride ions react with silver nitrate.

7. **In what industries is the limit test for chloride applicable?**

    - It is applicable in pharmaceutical, food, chemical, and environmental industries to control chloride levels.

8. **Why is controlling chloride levels important in pharmaceuticals?**

- Controlling chloride levels is important to prevent corrosion of equipment, degradation of active ingredients, and interference with the drug's therapeutic effect.

9. **What is the visual indicator of chloride presence in the limit test?**

   - The visual indicator is the formation of a white precipitate or turbidity in the solution.

10. **What is the role of the standard chloride solution in the test?**

   - The standard chloride solution is used as a reference to compare the intensity of the precipitate in the sample solution, determining if chloride levels are within acceptable limits

LIMIT TEST FOR SULPHATE

Principle:

Reaction between barium chloride and soluble sulphate in presence of dilute hydrochloric acid.

Then, the comparison of the turbidity produced by a given amount of the substance is done with a standard turbidity obtained from a known amount of sulphate and same volumes of dilute hydrochloric acid have been added to both the solutions.

$$BaCl_2 + Sulphate = BaSO_4 + Chloride$$
$$BaCl_2 + Na_2SO_4 = BaSO_4 + 2NaCl$$

Reasoning:

- Hydrochloric acid helps to make solution acidic.
- Potassium sulphate is used to increase the sensitivity of the test by giving ionic concentration in the reagent.

- Alcohol helps to prevent super saturation and so produces a more uniform opalescence

BARIUM SULPHATE REAGENTS:

S. No	Composition	Used
1.	15 ml of 0.5%BaCl$_2$	Used as precipitating agent
2.	20 ml of sulphate free alcohol	Used to prevent supersaturation
3.	5 ml of 0.01081% w/v Potassium sulphate	Used as seeding agent and to increase the ionic concentration and sensitivity of the test.
4.	Purified water quantity sufficient to 100 ml	Diluent

Procedure

Take two 50 ml Nessler Cylinders. Label one as "Test" and the other as 'Standard'.

S. No	Test	Standard
1.	Dissolve the sample in distilled water and transfer to a Nessler cylinder.	Place 1ml of 0.1089% w/v solution of
2.	Add 2 ml of dilute Hydrochloride acid.	Add 2 ml of dilute Hydrochloride acid.
3.	Dilute to45 ml with water and add 5ml of Barium sulphate reagent .	Dilute to45 ml with water and add 5ml of Barium sulphate reagent .
4.	Stir immediately with a glass rod and allow to stand for 5 minutes	Stir immediately with a glass rod and allow to stand for 5 minutes

Observation: The opalescence produce in sample solution should not be greater than standard solution. If opalescence produces in sample solution is less than the standard solution, the sample will pass the limit test of chloride and visa versa.

Questions and Answers on Limit Test for Sulfate

1. **What is the purpose of the limit test for sulfate in pharmaceuticals?**
   - The limit test for sulfate ensures that the sulfate content in pharmaceutical substances does not exceed specified limits to maintain product safety and quality.

2. **What principle is the limit test for sulfate based on?**
   - The principle is based on the formation of an insoluble barium sulfate precipitate when barium chloride reacts with sulfate ions in the sample.

3. **Which reagent is added to the sample to detect sulfate ions?**
   - Barium chloride ($BaCl_2$) is added to the sample to react with sulfate ions and form barium sulfate ($BaSO_4$) precipitate.

4. **Why is hydrochloric acid added to the sample solution before the barium chloride?**
   - Hydrochloric acid is added to prevent the precipitation of other barium salts and to ensure the reaction is specific to sulfate ions.

5. **How is the intensity of the precipitate compared in the limit test for sulfate?**
   - The intensity of the precipitate is compared visually or using instruments against a standard sulfate solution.

6. **What forms the white precipitate in the limit test for sulfate?**
   - The white precipitate is barium sulfate ($BaSO_4$), which forms when sulfate ions react with barium chloride.

7. **What is the visual indicator of sulfate presence in the limit test?**

- The visual indicator is the formation of a white precipitate or turbidity in the solution.

8. **What is the role of the standard sulfate solution in the test?**

   - The standard sulfate solution is used as a reference to compare the intensity of the precipitate in the sample solution, determining if sulfate levels are within acceptable limits.

9. **In which industries is the limit test for sulfate applicable?**

   - It is applicable in pharmaceutical, food, chemical, and environmental industries to control sulfate levels.

10. **Why is controlling sulfate levels important in pharmaceuticals?**

    - Controlling sulfate levels is important to prevent potential adverse effects on drug stability, safety, and efficacy.

MODIFIED LIMIT TEST FOR CHLORIDE

If the limit tests for sample (colour compound) cannot be done by normal method. Potassium permagnate is decolorized by boiling with ethanol, filter to remove precipitated magnesium dioxide and filtrate is subjected to the test

It is based on the reaction between silver nitrate and soluble chloride to obtain silver chloride which is insoluble in dilute nitric acid.

The silver chloride produced in the presence of dilute nitric acid makes the solution turbid, the extent of turbidity depends upon the amount of chloride present in the substance is compared with a standard opalescence produced by addition of silver nitrate to a standard solution having a known amount of chloride and the same amount of dilute nitric acid as used in the test solution.

If turbidity in test solution has been less than standard turbidity, then the sample passes the limit test.

$$NaCl + AgNO_3 \xrightarrow{\;HNO_3\;} AgCl + NaNO_3$$

Reasons:

- Nitric acid is added in the limit test of chloride to make solution acidic and helps silver chloride precipitate to make solution turbid at the end of process.
- This test is not use for immiscible solid.

Requirements:

- A pair of Nessler's cylinder
- Pipettes
- Measuring Cylinder
- Beakers
- Droppers
- Standard Sodium Chloride solution (Dilute 50 ml of 0.08245 g NaCl in 100 ml distilled water)
- Dil. Nitric Acid: dilute 1.06 ml of concentrated nitric acid sufficient distilled water to produce 100 ml.
- Silver nitrate Solution (0.1 M): Dissolve 1.7 gm of silver nitrate to 100 ml of distilled water.
- Ethyl alcohol
- Test sample (Potassium permagnate)

NOTE - The solutions used for this test should be prepared with distilled water

Procedure:

Preparation of test sample ($KMnO_4$): Dissolve 1.5 g in 50 ml of distilled water, heat on a water bath and add gradually 6 ml of ethanol (95%), cool, dilute to 60 ml with distilled water and filter.

S. No	Test sample	Standard
1.	Take 40 ml of the above test solution in Nessler cylinder	Take 10 ml of solution of sodium chloride(250 ppm of chloride) in 5 ml of water in

			Nessler cylinder B
2.	Add 1 ml Dil. Nitric acid	Add 1 ml Dil. Nitric acid
3.	Diluted to 50 ml. with distilled water in Nessler cylinder A	Diluted to 50 ml. with distilled water in Nessler cylinder B
4.	Add 1 ml of 0.1 M Silver Nitrate solution	Add 1 ml of 0.1 M Silver Nitrate solution
5.	Stir with glass rod & kept aside for 5 Minute.	Stir with glass rod & kept aside for 5 Minute.
6.	Observe the opalescence	Observe the opalescence

Modified limit test for sulphate:

From I.P. 1996 onwards, limit test for sulphate has been modified to a great extent. It has done away the requirement of barium sulphate reagent

CHAPTER – 4

LIMIT TEST FOR IRON AND ARSENIC

Mrs. Shaily Goyal

Associate Professor, Rajiv Gandhi Institute of Pharmacy, Faculty of Pharmaceutical Science & Technology, AKS University Satna, MP-India

ABSTRACT:

The limit tests for iron and arsenic are critical quality control procedures used to detect and quantify trace amounts of these impurities in pharmaceutical substances. These tests ensure that the levels of iron and arsenic do not exceed permissible limits, safeguarding the safety, efficacy, and quality of the products. The limit test for iron typically involves the reaction of iron with thioglycolic acid or ammonium thiocyanate in an acidic medium to form a colored complex, which is then compared against a standard solution. The limit test for arsenic, on the other hand, often employs the Gutzeit or Marsh test, where arsenic is converted to arsine gas and detected by its reaction with mercuric bromide paper, resulting in a yellow or brown stain. These tests are essential in the pharmaceutical industry to prevent toxic effects associated with iron and arsenic, which can lead to severe health issues. By adhering to standardized methods outlined in pharmacopeias, manufacturers can ensure their products meet regulatory requirements. Advanced analytical techniques like atomic absorption spectroscopy (AAS) and inductively coupled plasma mass spectrometry (ICP-MS) complement these classical methods, providing greater sensitivity and specificity in detecting these impurities.

LIMIT TEST FOR IRON

Principle:

Limit test of iron is based on the reaction iron with thioglycollic acid in the presence of ammonical solution and citric acid.

$$2HSCH_2COOH + Fe^{+2} \quad = \quad Fe(HSCH_2COO)_2 \ + 2H^+$$

Thioglycolic acid   Ferrous thioglycolic acid

A pale pink to deep reddish purple colour is formed due to the formation of ferrous compound. The coloured produced from the specified amount of substance from the test is compared with a standard (ferric ammonium sulphate).

Procedure:

S. No	Test	Standard
1.	Sample +40 ml of water	2 ml of standard solution of iron and dilute 40 ml distilled water
2.	2 ml of 20% w/v (iron free) citric acid	2 ml of 20% w/v (iron free) citric acid
3.	2 drop of thioglycolic acid ; solution mixed	2 drop of thioglycolic acid ; solution mixed
4.	made alkaline with ammonia volume adjusted to 50 ml ;	made alkaline with ammonia volume adjusted to 50 ml ;
5.	allowed to stand and color developed viewed vertically and compared with standard solution	allowed to stand and color developed viewed vertically and compared with standard solution

Observation:

The purple colour produce in sample solution should not be greater than standard solution. If purple colour produces in sample solution is less than the standard solution, the sample will pass the limit test of iron and vice versa.

Reasoning:

1. **Thioglycollic acid**

- Iron impurities may be present in the trivelant ferric form or in the divelent ferrous form. If it is present in ferric form then thioglycolic acid reduces it to the ferrous form.
- Thioglycolic acid produce purple colour with ferrous ion in the ammonical alkaline medium

2. **Citric acid:**

- Its prevent precipitation of iron with ammonia. It keeps iron in the solution form even in the presence of ammonia by forming a complex.

Or

- Citric acid forms complex with metal cation and helps precipitation of iron by ammonia by forming a complex with it.

3. **Ammonia:**

- Ammonia is added to make solution alkaline. The pale pink colour is visible only in the alkaline media. The colour is not visible in acidic media as ferrous thioglycolate complex decomposes in high acidic media.

Questions and Answers on Limit Test for Iron

1. **What is the purpose of the limit test for iron in pharmaceuticals?**

- The limit test for iron ensures that the iron content in pharmaceutical substances does not exceed specified limits to maintain product safety and quality.

2. **What principle is the limit test for iron based on?**

- The principle is based on the formation of a colored complex when iron reacts with thioglycolic acid or ammonium thiocyanate in an acidic medium.

3. **Which reagent is commonly used to detect iron ions in the limit test for iron?**

- Thioglycolic acid or ammonium thiocyanate is commonly used to detect iron ions.

4. **Why is an acidic medium used in the limit test for iron?**

   - An acidic medium is used to ensure that iron ions are in the correct oxidation state and to prevent interference from other metal ions.

5. **How is the intensity of the colored complex compared in the limit test for iron?**

   - The intensity of the colored complex is compared visually or using a colorimeter against a standard iron solution.

6. **What color does the iron complex exhibit in the limit test for iron?**

   - The iron complex typically exhibits a pink to red color.

7. **What is the visual indicator of iron presence in the limit test?**

   - The visual indicator is the intensity of the pink to red color formed in the solution.

8. **What is the role of the standard iron solution in the test?**

   - The standard iron solution is used as a reference to compare the intensity of the color in the sample solution, determining if iron levels are within acceptable limits.

9. **In which industries is the limit test for iron applicable?**

   - It is applicable in pharmaceutical, food, chemical, and environmental industries to control iron levels.

10. **Why is controlling iron levels important in pharmaceuticals?**

   - Controlling iron levels is important to prevent potential adverse effects on drug stability, safety, and efficacy.

LIMIT TEST OF ARSENIC

Arsenic is a well-known undesirable and harmful impurities, which is present in medicinal substance. All pharmacopoeias prescribe a limit test for it. The Pharmacopeial method is based on the **Gutzeit test.**

Principle of limit test for Arsenic:

1. Arsenic is the conversion of arsenic impurity to arsine gas which passed over $HgCl_2$ paper to form a yellow –brown stain. The intensity of the colour produced by sample is compared with that of the standard.

2. Arsenic present as an impurity is first converted to arsenic acid or arsenious acid in the presence of reducing system like $SnCl_2/HCl$.

3. The arsine gas is thus produced from arsenious acid in the presence of nascent hydrogen (Which is produced by Zn +HCl)

4. The use of KI ensure moderate and constant supply of nascent hydrogen

5. The arsine gas reacts with $HgCl_2$ paper to form a yellow brown stain owing to the formation of mercuric arsenide.

$$As^{3+} \xrightarrow[SnCl2]{HCl} As{\Big\langle}^{OH}_{-OH}_{OH} \quad (H_3AsO_3)$$

Trivalent arsenic

Arsenious acid

$$As^{+5} \xrightarrow[SnCl2]{HCl} O{=}As{\Big\langle}^{OH}_{-OH}_{OH} \quad (H_3AsO_4)$$

Pentavalent arsenic

Arsenic acid

$$H_3AsO_4 \xrightarrow{KI} H_3AsO_3$$

Arsenic acid

Arsenious acid

$$H_3AsO_3 \; + \; 3H_2 \longrightarrow AsH_3 \uparrow \; + 3H_2O$$

Arsenious acid

Nascent hydrogen

Arsine gas

$$2AsH_3 \; + HgCl_2 \longrightarrow Hg{\Big\langle}^{AsH_2}_{AsH_2} \; + 2HCl$$

Arsine gas

Mercuric chloride paper

Mercuric arsinide

Yellow –brown colour

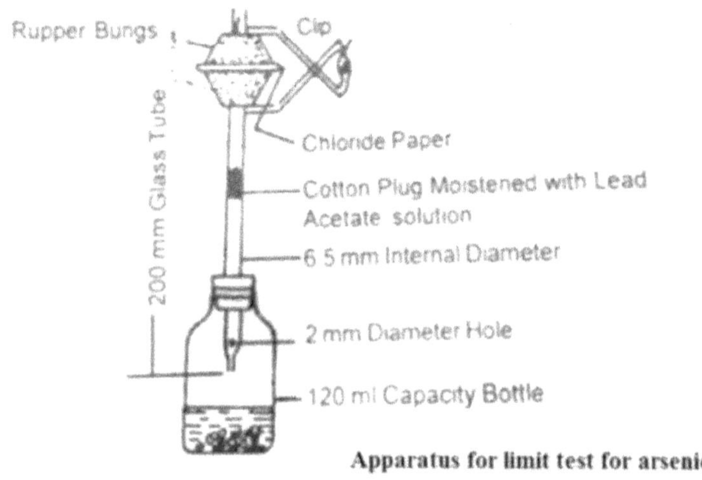

Apparatus for limit test for arsenic

Procedure:

S. No	Test	Standard
1.	The test solution is prepare by dissolving specific amount water and stannated HCl ((arsenic free) and kept in a wide mouthed bottle.	A known amount of dilute arsenic solution in water and stannated HCl ((arsenic free) and kept in a wide mouthed bottle
2.	1 g potassium iodide	1 g potassium iodide
3.	5 ml of stannous chloride acid solution	5 ml of stannous chloride acid solution
4.	10 gm of granulated zinc is added (arsenic free)	10 gm of granulated zinc is added (arsenic free)
5.	Keep the solution aside for 40 minutes	Keep the solution aside for 40 minutes

Observation:

- Stain obtained on mercuric chloride paper is compared with standard solution. Standard stain must be freshly prepared as it fades on keeping.

- Inference: If the stain produced by the test is not deeper than the standard stain, then sample complies with the limit test for Arsenic.

NOTE: If Evaluation hydrogen gas is very slow i.e. if the reaction is very slow, the two apparatus should be warmed to 40^0C by placing these in a warm place or in water bath at 40^0C.

Reasoning:

1. Potassium iodide is used because it help in the reduction of pentavelant arsenic acid to trivelent arsenic acid. Potassium iodide is first converted into hydroiodic acid (HI), which helps in this reduction process

2. Zinc granulated is used instead of ordinary zinc because evolution of nascent hydrogen is steady and prolonged with granulated zinc.

3. Stannous chloride is used for complete evolution of arsine.

4. Zinc, potassium iodide and stannous chloride is used as a reducing agent.

5. Hydrochloride acid is used to make the solution acidic.

6. Lead acetate paper are used to trap any hydrogen sulphide which may be evolved along with arsine.

7. Zinc granules usually contain traces of sulphate impurities. These impurities with react with nescent hydrogen forming hydrogen sulphide gas, which coming into contact with $HgCl_2$ paper gives a black stain (HgS). So , to prevent this interference, lead acetate cotton wool is used to drop hydrogen sulphide gas (H_2S) by converting it PbS in the glass tube itself.

$$Pb(CH_3COO)_2 \;+\; H_2S \uparrow \longrightarrow PbS \;+\; 2CH_3COOH$$

Lead acetate   Hydrogen sulphide gas   Lead sulphide

Questions and Answers

1. **Q:** What is the purpose of the limit test for arsenic?

   A: The purpose is to determine the presence and acceptable limit of arsenic in a sample.

2. **Q:** Which apparatus is commonly used in the limit test for arsenic?

   A: A Gutzeit apparatus or a Marsh apparatus is commonly used.

3. **Q:** What is the principle behind the limit test for arsenic?

   A: The principle is based on the conversion of arsenic to arsine gas, which reacts with mercuric chloride paper to form a yellow stain.

4. **Q:** Which reagent is used to generate arsine gas in the limit test for arsenic?

   A: Zinc in acid solution is used to generate arsine gas from arsenic.

5. **Q:** How is the intensity of the yellow stain on mercuric chloride paper interpreted? **A:** The intensity of the yellow stain is compared to a standard stain produced under similar conditions to determine if the sample meets the acceptable limit.

6. **Q:** Why is hydrochloric acid used in the limit test for arsenic?

   A: Hydrochloric acid is used to dissolve the sample and provide the acidic conditions necessary for the generation of arsine gas.

7. **Q:** What role does potassium iodide play in the limit test for arsenic?

   A: Potassium iodide acts as a reducing agent to ensure the complete conversion of arsenic to arsine gas.

8. **Q:** What is the acceptable limit of arsenic in pharmaceutical substances according to the test?

   A: The acceptable limit varies but is generally around 1 ppm (parts per million).

9. **Q:** What is the appearance of a positive result in the limit test for arsenic?

   A: A positive result is indicated by a yellow stain on the mercuric chloride paper.

10.**Q:** Why is it important to compare the test stain with a standard stain in the limit test for arsenic?

A: Comparing the test stain with a standard ensures that the test results are accurate and reliable, as the intensity of the color indicates the concentration of arsenic.

CHAPTER – 5

LIMIT TEST FOR HEAVY METAL AND LEAD

Mr. Prabhakar Tiwari

Associate Professor, Rajiv Gandhi Institute of Pharmacy, Faculty of

Pharmaceutical Science & Technology, AKS University, Satna, MP-India

ABSTRACT:

The limit tests for heavy metals and lead are crucial analytical procedures in the pharmaceutical industry to ensure that these toxic contaminants are within safe limits in drug substances and products. Heavy metals, including lead, can be introduced during manufacturing processes or from raw materials and can pose significant health risks if ingested in large amounts. The limit test for heavy metals typically involves treating the sample with a reagent, such as thioacetamide, which forms a colored complex with heavy metals. The intensity of the resulting color is compared to a standard solution. For lead, the test usually involves the reaction with hydrogen sulfide to form a black precipitate of lead sulfide, which is then compared to a standard lead solution. These tests help ensure compliance with regulatory standards set by bodies like the USP and EP. The presence of heavy metals and lead is closely monitored because their accumulation in the body can cause severe health issues, including neurological, renal, and cardiovascular problems. Advanced techniques like atomic absorption spectroscopy (AAS) and inductively coupled plasma mass spectrometry (ICP-MS) are also used for more precise quantification. Implementing these tests ensures the safety, efficacy, and quality of pharmaceutical products, protecting consumer health.

LIMIT TEST FOR HEAVY METAL

Principle:

It based on the reaction between hydrogen sulphide and heavy metals in an acidic medium to produce the metal sulphides. These remain distributed in a colloidal state and produce brownish colouration. The test solution is compared with a standard prepared using solution of lead nitrate (as Heavy metal).

$$\text{Heavy metal} + H_2S \xrightarrow{\text{Acidic medium}} \text{Sulphides of heavy metals (Brown colour)}$$

$$Pb^{+2} + H_2S \longrightarrow PbS \downarrow + H^+$$

Note: Metals that response to this test are lead, mercury, bismuth, arsenic, antimony, tin, cadmium, silver, copper, and molybdenum. The metallic impurities in substances are expressed as parts of lead per million parts of the substance. The usual limit as per Indian Pharmacopoeia is 20 ppm

Procedure:

As Indian Pharmacopoeia, three methods for the limit test of heavy metals.

Method-A: substance which gives clear colorless solution

S. No	Test sample	Standard
1.	Solution is prepared as per the monograph and 25 ml is transferred in Nessler's cylinder	Take 2 ml of standard lead solution and dilute to 25 ml with water
2.	Adjust the pH between 3 to 4 by adding dilute acetic acid or dilute ammonia solution 'Sp'	Adjust the pH between 3 to 4 by adding dilute acetic acid or dilute ammonia solution
3.	Dilute with water to 35 ml	Dilute with water to 35 ml
4.	Add freshly prepared 10 ml of hydrogen sulphide solution	Add freshly prepared 10 ml of hydrogen sulphide solution
5.	Dilute with water to 50 ml	Dilute with water to 50 ml

| 6. | Allow to stand for five minutes | Allow to stand for five minutes |
| 7. | View downwards over a white surface | View downwards over a white surface |

Observation: The color produce in sample solution should not be greater than standard solution

Method II: Use for the substance which do not give clear colorless solution under the specific condition.

S. No	Test sample	Standard
1.	Weigh specific quantity of test substance, moisten with sulphuric acid and ignite on a low flame till completely charred. Add few drops of nitric acid and heat to 500 °C Allow to cool and add 4 ml of hydrochloric acid and evaporate to dryness. Moisten the residue with 10 ml of hydrochloric acid and digest for two minutes. Neutralize with ammonia solution and make just acid with acetic acid	Take 2 ml of standard lead solution and dilute to 25 ml with water
2.	Adjust the pH between 3 to 4 and filter if necessary	Adjust the pH between 3 to 4 by adding dilute acetic acid 'Sp' or dilute ammonia solution 'Sp'
3.	Dilute with water to 35 ml	Dilute with water to 35 ml
4.	Add freshly prepared 10 ml of hydrogen sulphide solution	Add freshly prepared 10 ml of hydrogen sulphide

S. No	Test sample	Standard
		solution
5.	Dilute with water to 50 ml	Dilute with water to 50 ml
6.	Allow to stand for five minutes	Allow to stand for five minutes
7.	View downwards over a white surface	View downwards over a white surface

Observation: The color produce in sample solution should not be greater than standard solution.

Method III: the substance which gives clear colorless solution in sodium hydroxide solution

S. No	Test sample	Standard
1.	Solution is prepared as per the monograph and 25 ml is transferred in Nessler's cylinder or weigh specific amount of substance and dissolve in 20 ml of water and add 5 ml of dilute sodium hydroxide solution	Take 2 ml of standard lead solution
2.	Make up the volume to 50 ml with water	Add 5 ml of dilute sodium hydroxide solution and make up the volume to 50 ml with water
3.	Add 5 drops of sodium sulphide solution	Add 5 drops of sodium sulphide solution
4.	Mix and set aside for 5 min	Mix and set aside for 5 min
5.	View downwards over a white surface	View downwards over a white surface

LIMIT TEST FOR LEAD

Principle:

It is the reaction between lead and dithizone (Diphenylthiocarbazone) to form a complex. A chloroform solution of dithizone is prepared, which can extract led from alkaline aqueous solution as lead dithiozone complex (red in colour). The original colour of dithizone in chloroform is green while the lead-dithizonate complex is violet in colour. The intensity of the violet colour of the complex depending upon the quantity of lead present in the solution is compared with standard colour produced by standard solution.

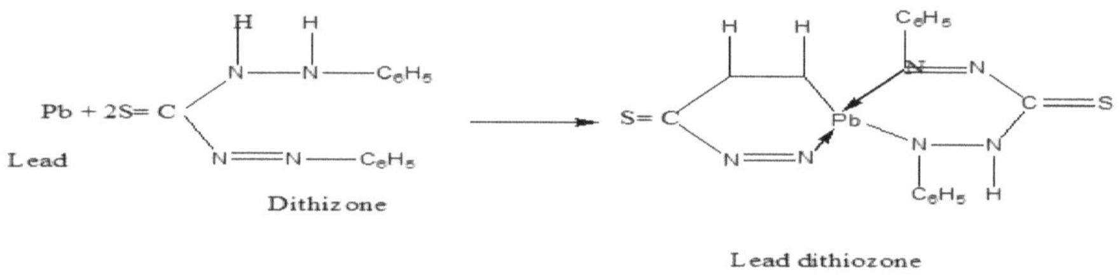

Requirements:

- A pair of Nesslers cylinder
- Pipettes
- Measuring Cylinder
- Beakers
- Dropper
- Glass rods
- Ammonium citrate
- Potassium cyanide
- Hydroxylamine hydrochloride
- Phenol red
- Dithizone
- Ammonia solution.

NOTE - The solutions used for this test should be prepared with distilled water.

S	Test sample	Standard
1.	A known quantity of sample solution is transferred in a separating funnel	A standard lead solution is prepared equivalent to the amount of lead permitted in the sample under examination
2.	Add 6ml of ammonium citrate	Add 6ml of ammonium citrate
3.	Add 2 ml of potassium cyanide and 2 ml of hydroxylamine hydrochloride	Add 2 ml of potassium cyanide and 2 ml of hydroxylamine hydrochloride
4.	Make solution alkaline by adding ammonia solution.	Make solution alkaline by adding ammonia solution.
5.	Extract with 5 ml of dithizone until it becomes green	Extract with 5 ml of dithizone until it becomes green
6.	Combine dithizone extracts are shaken for 30 mins with 30 ml of nitric acid and the chloroform layer is discarded	Combine dithizone extracts are shaken for 30 mins with 30 ml of nitric acid and the chloroform layer is discarded
7.	To the acid solution add 5 ml of standard dithizone solution	To the acid solution add 5 ml of standard dithizone solution
8.	To the acid solution add 5 ml of standard dithizone solution	To the acid solution add 5 ml of standard dithizone solution
9.	Add 4 ml of ammonium cyanide	Add 4 ml of ammonium cyanide
10.	Shake for 30 mins	Shake for 30 mins
11.	Observe the color	Observe the color

Questions and Answers on Limit Test for Heavy Metals and Lead

1. **What is the purpose of the limit test for heavy metals in pharmaceuticals?**
   - The limit test for heavy metals ensures that the levels of toxic heavy metals in pharmaceutical substances do not exceed specified limits, ensuring product safety and quality.

2. **What reagent is commonly used in the limit test for heavy metals?**
   - Thioacetamide is commonly used to form a colored complex with heavy metals in the test.

3. **What is the principle of the limit test for heavy metals?**
   - The principle is based on the formation of a colored complex between heavy metals and a reagent, which is then compared to a standard solution for intensity.

4. **How is the intensity of the color compared in the limit test for heavy metals?**
   - The intensity of the color is compared visually or using a colorimeter against a standard solution containing a known amount of heavy metals.

5. **What is the visual indicator of heavy metal presence in the limit test?**
   - The visual indicator is the intensity of the color formed in the solution.

6. **What reagent is used in the limit test for lead?**
   - Hydrogen sulfide (H_2S) is used to react with lead and form a black precipitate of lead sulfide.

7. **How is the presence of lead detected in the limit test for lead?**
   - The presence of lead is detected by the formation of a black precipitate of lead sulfide, which is then compared to a standard lead solution.

8. **Why is controlling the levels of heavy metals and lead important in pharmaceuticals?**

   o   Controlling these levels is important to prevent potential health risks, including neurological, renal, and cardiovascular problems.

9. **Which advanced techniques are used for precise quantification of heavy metals and lead?**

   o   Atomic absorption spectroscopy (AAS) and inductively coupled plasma mass spectrometry (ICP-MS) are used for precise quantification.

10. **In which industries are the limit tests for heavy metals and lead applicable?**

   o   These tests are applicable in pharmaceutical, food, chemical, and environmental industries to ensure safety and compliance with regulatory standards.

CHAPTER – 6

ACIDS, BASES AND BUFFERS

Mrs. Priyanka Gupta

Associate Professor, Rajiv Gandhi Institute of Pharmacy, Faculty of Pharmaceutical Science & Technology, AKS University Satna, MP-India

ABSTRACT:

Acids and bases are fundamental concepts in chemistry, with various theories explaining their behaviors and properties. The Arrhenius theory, proposed by Svante Arrhenius, defines acids as substances that increase the concentration of hydrogen ions (H^+) in aqueous solutions, while bases increase hydroxide ions (OH^-). This theory, although useful, is limited to aqueous solutions. The Brønsted-Lowry theory, developed by Johannes Brønsted and Thomas Lowry, expands on this by defining acids as proton donors and bases as proton acceptors, which applies to a broader range of chemical reactions beyond aqueous solutions. The Lewis theory, introduced by Gilbert N. Lewis, further broadens the definition by identifying acids as electron pair acceptors and bases as electron pair donors. This theory encompasses a wider variety of chemical species and reactions, including those that do not involve protons. Each theory provides unique insights into the behavior of acids and bases, enhancing our understanding of chemical reactivity and guiding practical applications in fields such as industrial chemistry, biochemistry, and environmental science. The interplay between these theories illustrates the evolution of scientific thought and the importance of multiple perspectives in developing a comprehensive understanding of complex phenomena.

Acids and Bases Theories with Examples

1. Traditional Theory / Concept

Traditional Theory classifies substances based on their taste and effect on litmus paper:

- **Acids**: Substances that taste sour and turn blue litmus paper red.
    - Example: **Hydrochloric Acid (HCl)**
        - Sour taste, turns blue litmus red.
- **Bases**: Substances that taste bitter and turn red litmus paper blue.
    - Example: **Sodium Hydroxide (NaOH)**
        - Bitter taste, turns red litmus blue.

2. Arrhenius Theory

Arrhenius Theory defines acids and bases in terms of their dissociation in water:

- **Acids**: Substances that dissociate in water to produce hydrogen ions (H^+).
    - Example: **Sulfuric Acid (H_2SO_4)**
        - Dissociates in water: $H_2SO_4 \rightarrow 2H^+ + SO_4^{2-}$
- **Bases**: Substances that dissociate in water to produce hydroxide ions (OH^-).
    - Example: **Potassium Hydroxide (KOH)**
        - Dissociates in water: $KOH \rightarrow K^+ + OH^-$

3. Bronsted and Lowry Theory

Bronsted-Lowry Theory focuses on proton transfer:

- **Acids**: Proton donors (H^+ donors).
    - Example: **Nitric Acid (HNO_3)**
        - Donates a proton: $HNO_3 \rightarrow H^+ + NO_3^-$

- **Bases**: Proton acceptors (H^+ acceptors).
  - Example: **Ammonia (NH_3)**
    - Accepts a proton: $NH_3 + H^+ \rightarrow NH_4^+$

4. Lewis Theory

Lewis Theory defines acids and bases in terms of electron pair exchange:

- **Acids**: Electron pair acceptors.
  - Example: **Boron Trifluoride (BF_3)**
    - Accepts an electron pair: $BF_3 + NH_3 \rightarrow BF_3$
- **Bases**: Electron pair donors.
  - Example: **Ammonia (NH_3)**
    - Donates an electron pair: $NH_3 + H^+ \rightarrow NH_4^+$

Summary Table

Theory / Concept	Acid Example	Base Example	Definition / Characteristic
Traditional Theory	Hydrochloric Acid (HCl)	Sodium Hydroxide (NaOH)	Acids taste sour and turn blue litmus red; Bases taste bitter and turn red litmus blue
Arrhenius Theory	Sulfuric Acid (H_2SO_4)	Potassium Hydroxide (KOH)	Acids produce H^+ ions in water; Bases produce OH^- ions in water
Bronsted-Lowry Theory	Nitric Acid (HNO_3)	Ammonia (NH_3)	Acids are proton donors (H^+); Bases are proton acceptors (H^+)
Lewis Theory	Boron Trifluoride	Ammonia (NH_3)	Acids are electron pair acceptors; Bases are electron

Theory / Concept	Acid Example	Base Example	Definition / Characteristic
	(BF_3)		pair donors

Limitations:

1. Water is essential
2. It is not explain acidity or basicity of Non aqueous Solvent. Eg :benzene
3. Basicity of Ammonia (No OH^- ion) is not explained.
4. Acidity of BF_3, $AlCl_3$ (No H^+ ion) is not explained.
5. Acidity of oxides of P block element (CO_2) is not explained.
6. Basicity of oxides of S- block element (Na_2O) is not explained.
7. Neutralization without absence of solvent is not explained.

3. Lowry Bronsted theory:

- Proton theory of acids and bases
- In 1923 the Danish chemist Johannes Nicolaus Bronsted and the English chemist Thomas Martin Lowry, proposed the theory
- Acid: Acid is the substance which donate proton
- Base: Base is the substance which accept proton.

4. Lewis theory:

- In 1923 of scientist G.N. Lewis proposed the theory in terms of chemical structure
- Acid: acid is the molecule or ion that accepts the lone pair of electrons. Example: H^+, $NH4^+$, Na^+, Cu^{+2}, Al^{+3}

- Base: Base is the molecule or ion that donates the lone pair of electrons. Example: OH⁻, Cl⁻, CN⁻

BUFFERS

A **buffer** is a solution that can resist pH change upon the addition of acidic or basic components.

It is able to neutralize small amounts of added acid or base, thus maintaining the pH of the solution relatively stable. This is important for processes and/or reactions which require specific and stable pH ranges

Buffer system: A buffer system can be made of a weak acid and its salt or a weak base and its salt. Example of a weak acid based buffer is acetic acid: (CH_3COOH) and sodium acetate (CH_3COONa). A common weak base buffer is made of ammonia (NH_3) and ammonium chloride (NH_4Cl).

Types of buffers:

1. **Acidic buffers**-It is combination of weak acid and its corresponding salt. Example: Mixture of acetic acid, sodium acetate
2. **Basic buffers-** buffers-It is combination of weak base and its corresponding salt. Example: Mixture of Ammonium hydroxide and ammonium chloride
3. **Neutral buffers:** It is single substance showing properties of buffers. Ex. Ammonium acetate

Buffer Capacity: It is defined as moles of strong acid or strong base required to change the pH of 1 lit. solution by 1 unit.

Properties of Buffer:

1. The pH of buffer solution is constant.
2. The pH does not change with dilution.

3. The pH does not changes with even after addition of small quantities of acid or bases

Factors for selection of Buffer:

When selecting a buffer for a particular application, several factors must be considered to ensure the buffer meets the required criteria. Here are the key factors:

1. **pH Range**: The buffer should have a pKa close to the desired pH of the solution, as buffers are most effective within ± 1 pH unit of their pKa.

2. **Buffer Capacity**: The ability of the buffer to resist changes in pH upon addition of acid or base. This is influenced by the concentration of the buffering species.

3. **Compatibility**: The buffer must be chemically compatible with other components in the solution and should not interfere with the chemical or biological processes being studied.

4. **Temperature Stability**: The buffer should maintain its buffering capacity and pH stability over the range of temperatures at which it will be used.

5. **Ionic Strength**: Consider the ionic strength of the buffer, which can affect the activity of biomolecules and the outcome of biochemical reactions.

6. **Solubility**: The buffer components should be soluble in the desired solvent at the required concentrations.

7. **Minimal Interference**: The buffer should not absorb significantly in the UV or visible spectrum if spectrophotometric measurements are involved, nor should it interfere with assays or reactions.

8. **Biological Compatibility**: For biological applications, the buffer should be non-toxic and not affect cell viability or function.

9. **Availability and Cost**: The buffer components should be readily available and cost-effective for the intended scale of use.

10. **Ease of Preparation**: The buffer should be easy to prepare and maintain, with clear instructions on the correct concentrations and adjustments needed.

11. **Reactivity**: The buffer should be inert and not participate in or catalyze side reactions that could interfere with the experiment or process.

Role of buffer:

- The buffers are in pharmaceutical preparation to ensure the stable pH conditions for medicinal active compounds
- Solubility of many compounds is controlled by providing by suitable pH.
- Color of many compounds is pH dependent.
- pH gives stability to different preparations.
- It provides patient comfort.
- Penicillin preparations are stabilized by addition of carbonates.
- Citric acid is used for stabilizing milk magnesia

Henderson Hassel batch Equation:

$$pH = pKa + \log \frac{[\text{conjugate base}]}{\text{weak base}]} \quad (\text{For weak acid})$$

$$pH = pKb + \log \frac{[\text{conjugate base}]}{\text{weak base}]} \quad (\text{For weak base})$$

The principal objectives of the Henderson Hasselbalch equation include the following:

The Henderson-Hasselbalch equation is a fundamental relationship in acid-base chemistry, and its principal objectives include:

1. pH Calculation: It allows for the calculation of the pH of a buffer solution based on the concentrations of the acid and its conjugate base (or base and its conjugate acid).

2. Buffer Preparation: It aids in the preparation of buffer solutions with a desired pH by determining the appropriate ratio of acid to conjugate base (or base to conjugate acid).

3. Understanding Buffer Capacity: It provides insights into the buffer capacity and how the pH of the solution changes with the addition of small amounts of acid or base.

4. Predicting pH Changes: It helps predict how the pH of a solution will change when the concentrations of the acid or base are altered, which is crucial for maintaining stable pH conditions in various chemical and biological processes.

5. pKa Determination: By rearranging the equation, the pKa of an acid can be determined if the pH and the concentrations of the acid and conjugate base are known.

6. Analysis of Acid-Base Equilibria: It facilitates the analysis and understanding of acid-base equilibria in aqueous solutions, contributing to broader applications in chemistry, biology, and medicine.

The Henderson-Hasselbalch equation is expressed as:

$$pH = pKa + \log\left(\frac{[A^-]}{[HA]}\right)$$

where:

- pH is the measure of acidity/basicity of the solution.
- pKa is the acid dissociation constant.
- $[A^-]$ is the concentration of the conjugate base.
- $[HA]$ is the concentration of the weak acid.

Principle/Theory/Derivation of Henderson Hasselbalch Equation:

- According to the Bronsted-Lowry theory of acids and bases, an acid (HA) can donate a proton (H^+) while a base (B) can accept a proton.
- An acid after losing a proton forms a conjugate base (A^-), and the protonated base exists as conjugate acid (BH^+).
- The dissociation of acid is expressed in terms of the equilibrium equation as:

$$HA \quad \leftrightarrow \quad H^+ + A^-$$

- This relationship can be described in terms of the equilibrium constant as:

$$Ka = \frac{[H^+ A^-]}{[HA]}$$

Now, take negative log on both sides of the equation gives:

$$-logKa = -log \frac{[H+ A-]}{[HA]}$$

Or

$$-logKa = -logH+ \; + \; (-log \frac{[A-]}{[HA]} \;)$$

By definition

$$-logKa = pKa \text{ and } -log[H^+] = pH$$

Thus

$$pKa = pH - log \frac{[A^-]}{[HA]}$$

This equation is than arranges to form the HAB equation as:

$$pH = pKa - log \frac{[A^-]}{[HA]}$$

The henderson Hasselbatch equation can be expressed :

$$pH = pKa + \log \frac{[\text{conjugate base}]}{[\text{weak base}]} \quad \text{(For weak acid)}$$

$$pOH = pKb + \log \frac{[\text{conjugate base}]}{[\text{weak base}]} \quad \text{(For weak acid)}$$

Where pKa = dissociation constant of acid

pKb = dissociation of base

Applications of Henderson Hasselbalch Equation

The Henderson-Hasselbalch equation has a wide range of applications in various scientific and industrial fields. Here are some of the key applications:

1. **Buffer Solution Preparation**:
   a. **Biological Buffers**: Used to prepare buffer solutions in biological experiments to maintain the pH of the environment for enzymes and other biomolecules.
   b. **Chemical Buffers**: Essential in chemical synthesis and reactions where pH control is crucial for the desired reaction pathways.
2. **Clinical and Medical Applications**:
   a. **Blood pH Regulation**: Helps in understanding and managing conditions related to acid-base imbalances in the human body, such as acidosis and alkalosis.
   b. **Pharmacology**: Assists in the formulation of pharmaceuticals to ensure drug stability and optimal absorption, which can be pH-dependent.
3. **Environmental Science**:
   a. **Water Treatment**: Used to design and control processes in water treatment plants to maintain the pH of water within safe and regulatory limits.

b. **Soil Chemistry**: Assists in managing soil pH for agricultural purposes, ensuring optimal conditions for plant growth and nutrient availability.

4. **Industrial Applications**:

   a. **Food and Beverage Industry**: Important in the preparation and preservation of food products where pH affects flavor, texture, and shelf life.

   b. **Cosmetics**: Helps in formulating skincare and cosmetic products to ensure they are within a pH range that is safe and effective for use on the skin.

5. **Research and Development**:

   a. **Biochemical Assays**: Used to maintain stable pH conditions in various assays and experiments in biochemistry and molecular biology.

   b. **Enzyme Kinetics**: Important for studying enzyme activities, as enzyme function is highly dependent on the pH of the environment.

6. **Educational Use**:

   a. **Teaching Tool**: Widely used in educational settings to teach concepts of acid-base chemistry, buffer systems, and pH control in various scientific disciplines.

7. **Electrochemistry**:

   a. **pH Sensors and Electrodes**: Helps in calibrating pH sensors and electrodes by providing standard buffer solutions with known pH values.

8. **Microbiology**:

   a. **Culture Media**: Used in the preparation of culture media for growing microorganisms, ensuring the pH is optimal for the growth and proliferation of specific microbes.

9. **Calculating the pH of a solution using pK$_a$:** This equation can be used to determine the pH of different solutions in different chemical equations as well as in biological systems like enzymes and proteins.

10. **Calculating the ionized and unionized concentrations of chemicals"**

- One of the most potent applications of the Henderson Hasselbalch equation is the ability to determine the concentrations of ionized and unionized chemicals.

- Generally, the amount of ionized and unionized species is detected using some spectroscopic technique, and thus, this equation is useful in the condition where spectroscopic studies are not feasible.

- The knowledge of the concentration of ionized and unionized chemicals is essential in fields like organic chemistry, analytical chemistry, and pharmaceuticals sciences,

11. **Calculating pK$_a$ of a molecule using pH**

- Determining the pK$_a$ of a molecule is important as the pK$_a$ is an essential characteristic of the chemistry of the structure of the molecule.

- Henderson Hasselbalch equation can be used to determine the pK$_a$ when the ratio of ionized and unionized forms and the pH of the solution is known.

12. **Determination of solubility**

- It has been observed that the Henderson Hasselbalch equation is important in determining the pH dependency of solubility.

- Based on the pH of a solution, the solubility of the solution can be determined, and there is also a close relationship between pH and solubility of various components in a solution.

13. **Calculating the isoelectric point of protein:** This equation can also be used in determining the isoelectric point of different proteins (pH at which proteins neither lose or accept protons).

Factors of some importance in the choice of Pharmaceutical buffer include:

Selecting a buffer for pharmaceutical applications requires careful consideration of several factors to ensure the buffer is appropriate for the drug formulation and its intended use. Key factors include:

1. **pH Range and Stability**:
   - The buffer should maintain a stable pH within the desired range, which is typically close to the physiological pH (around 7.4) for many pharmaceutical formulations.
   - Stability over the product's shelf life is crucial to maintain efficacy and safety.

2. **Buffer Capacity**:
   - Adequate buffer capacity is needed to resist changes in pH due to factors such as dilution, degradation, or interaction with other components in the formulation.

3. **Compatibility with Active Pharmaceutical Ingredients (APIs)**:
   - The buffer should not interact with the API in a way that affects its stability, solubility, or efficacy.
   - Compatibility with excipients and other formulation components is also important.

4. **Toxicity and Safety**:
   - The buffer components should be non-toxic and safe for the intended route of administration (oral, injectable, topical, etc.).
   - Regulatory approval and guidelines should be considered when selecting buffer components.

5. **Ionic Strength and Osmolarity**:
   - The buffer should maintain appropriate ionic strength and osmolarity, especially for injectable and ophthalmic formulations, to ensure compatibility with body fluids and avoid irritation or adverse reactions.

6. **Solubility**:

o The buffer components should be highly soluble in the solvent used in the formulation to avoid precipitation and ensure uniform distribution.

7. **Biocompatibility**:

o For formulations that come into contact with biological tissues (e.g., injectables, ophthalmic solutions), the buffer should be biocompatible and not cause irritation, inflammation, or other adverse effects.

8. **pH Control and Release Kinetics**:

o The buffer should maintain pH control over the release period of the drug, ensuring consistent delivery and bioavailability.

9. **Temperature Stability**:

o The buffer should be stable across a range of temperatures, especially for formulations that may be exposed to varying storage or transportation conditions.

10. **Regulatory Compliance**:

o Buffer components should be compliant with regulatory standards and guidelines set by agencies such as the FDA, EMA, or other relevant authorities.

o Documentation and quality control measures should be in place to ensure consistency and compliance.

11. **Cost and Availability**:

o The buffer components should be readily available and cost-effective, considering the scale of production and commercial viability.

12. **Effect on Drug Delivery Systems**:

o For advanced drug delivery systems (e.g., controlled release, nanoparticles), the buffer should not adversely affect the delivery mechanism or the stability of the delivery system.

General Procedures for Preparing Pharmaceutical Buffer Solutions:

Preparing pharmaceutical buffer solutions involves several key steps to ensure accuracy, consistency, and safety. Below are the general procedures for preparing such buffer solutions:

1. Determine the Desired pH and Buffer Capacity

- **Identify the pH Range**: Select the target pH based on the application and the stability requirements of the drug formulation.
- **Buffer Capacity**: Decide on the buffer capacity needed to resist pH changes, considering the formulation's exposure to acids, bases, or other pH-altering substances.

2. Select Appropriate Buffer System

- **Buffer Components**: Choose suitable acid and conjugate base pair (or base and conjugate acid pair) that have a pKa close to the desired pH.
- **Compatibility**: Ensure the selected buffer components are compatible with the active pharmaceutical ingredient (API) and other excipients.

3. Calculate the Required Amounts of Buffer Components

- **Henderson-Hasselbalch Equation**: Use the equation to calculate the ratio of the buffer components needed to achieve the desired pH.
- **Molarity**: Decide on the concentration of the buffer solution to ensure adequate buffer capacity.

4. Prepare the Stock Solutions

- **Weighing and Dissolving**: Accurately weigh the required amounts of buffer components and dissolve them in a small volume of distilled or deionized water.
- **Mixing**: Prepare separate stock solutions for the acid and base components if needed.

5. Adjust the pH

- **Combine Solutions**: Mix the acid and conjugate base solutions in the calculated ratio.
- **pH Meter Calibration**: Calibrate the pH meter using standard pH calibration solutions before measuring the pH of the buffer solution.
- **Fine-tuning**: Adjust the pH by adding small amounts of acid or base (preferably the components of the buffer system) until the desired pH is achieved.

6. Dilute to Final Volume

- **Volume Adjustment**: Dilute the buffer solution to the final desired volume with distilled or deionized water.
- **Mix Thoroughly**: Ensure thorough mixing to achieve a homogenous buffer solution.

7. Sterilization (if necessary)

- **Filtration**: Use a 0.22-micron filter to sterilize the buffer solution if required for sterile applications.
- **Autoclaving**: Alternatively, autoclave the buffer solution if the components are heat-stable.

8. Quality Control and Testing

- **pH Measurement**: Recheck the pH of the final buffer solution to ensure it meets the specified range.
- **Documentation**: Record the formulation details, pH measurements, and any adjustments made during preparation.
- **Stability Testing**: Perform stability testing to ensure the buffer maintains its pH over time under storage conditions.

9. Storage

- **Container Selection**: Store the buffer solution in appropriate, labeled containers (e.g., glass or plastic bottles) that are compatible with the buffer components.

- **Conditions**: Store under specified conditions (e.g., temperature, light protection) to maintain stability and prevent contamination.

Example Preparation of a Phosphate Buffer Solution (pH 7.4)

1. **Determine Required pH and Buffer Capacity**:
   - Target pH: 7.4
   - Desired buffer capacity for pharmaceutical use.

2. **Select Buffer System**:
   - Sodium phosphate monobasic (NaH_2PO_4) and sodium phosphate dibasic (Na^2HPO_4).

3. **Calculate Required Amounts**:
   - Using the Henderson-Hasselbalch equation, determine the ratio of NaH2PO4 to Na2HPO4 for pH 7.4.

4. **Prepare Stock Solutions**:
   - Dissolve calculated amounts of NaH_2PO_4 and Na_2HPO_4 in distilled water.

5. **Adjust the pH**:
   - Mix the solutions and adjust the pH by adding more of either component if needed.

6. **Dilute to Final Volume**:
   - Dilute the mixed solution to the desired final volume with distilled water.

7. **Sterilization** (if required):
   - Filter the solution using a 0.22-micron filter.

8. **Quality Control and Testing**:
   - Verify the pH and document the process.

9. **Storage**:
   - Store the buffer in labeled containers under appropriate conditions.

Stability of buffer:

The stability of a buffer solution is a critical aspect to consider in various applications, particularly in pharmaceuticals, biological research, and industrial processes. Several factors influence the stability of a buffer:

1. **pH Range**: Buffers are most stable within their effective pH range, typically within one pH unit of the pKa of the buffering agent. Outside this range, the buffer's ability to resist changes in pH diminishes significantly.

2. **Concentration**: Higher concentrations of buffer components can enhance stability by providing a greater capacity to neutralize added acids or bases. However, very high concentrations may lead to issues such as precipitation or changes in ionic strength.

3. **Temperature**: Temperature changes can affect the dissociation constants (pKa) of the buffering agents, altering the buffer's pH. It is essential to maintain a constant temperature or to choose buffers that are less sensitive to temperature fluctuations.

4. **Ionic Strength**: The presence of other ions in the solution can influence the stability of the buffer by affecting the activity coefficients of the buffer components. Maintaining a consistent ionic strength is crucial for stable buffer performance.

5. **Chemical Compatibility**: Buffers must be chemically compatible with all other components in the solution, including solvents, solutes, and container materials. Incompatible substances can react with buffer components, leading to degradation or precipitation.

6. **Microbial Growth**: In biological and pharmaceutical applications, microbial contamination can degrade buffer components, alter pH, and compromise the solution's sterility. Sterilization and the use of preservatives can help mitigate this risk.

7. **Light and Air Exposure**: Some buffer components are sensitive to light and air, which can lead to oxidation or photodegradation. Storing buffer solutions in opaque, airtight containers can help maintain their stability.

8. **Shelf Life**: Over time, buffer components may degrade, even under optimal storage conditions. Regular testing and validation are necessary to ensure the buffer maintains its desired properties throughout its intended shelf life.

9. **Contamination**: Contaminants introduced during preparation or use can affect the stability and effectiveness of the buffer. Using high-purity reagents, clean equipment, and sterile techniques can help prevent contamination.

10. **pH Measurement and Adjustment**: Accurate pH measurement and careful adjustment during buffer preparation are crucial. Calibration of pH meters and proper handling of pH adjustment reagents ensure the buffer starts with the correct pH.

ISOTONICITY SOLUTION

Two solutions having the same osmotic pressure across a semipermeable membrane is referred to as an isotonic solution. It has the same osmolality (solute concentration), as another solution. A solution is isotonic when its effective osmole concentration is the same as that of another solution. This state provides the free movement of water across the membrane without changing the concentration of solutes on either side. Some examples of isotonic solutions are 0.9% normal saline and lactated ringers.

ISOTONIC SOLUTION:

1. A solution containing 0.9% of sodium chloride is practically isotonic with blood plasma and is regarded as standard.

2. A solution containing more than 0.9% sodium chloride is called 'hypertonic'.

3. A solution containing less than 0.9% sodium chloride is called 'hypotonic'.

The need to achieve isotonic conditions with solutions to be applied to delicate membranes is dramatically illustrated by mixing a small quantity of blood with aqueous sodium chloride solutions of varying tonicity.

a. **Isotonic:** if a small quantity of blood is mixed with a solution containing 0.9 g of NaCl per 100 mL, the cells retain their normal size. The solution has essentially the same salt concentration and hence the same osmotic pressure as the red blood cell contents

b. **Hypertonic:** If the red blood cells are suspended in a 2.0% NaCl solution, the water within the cells passes through the cell membrane in an attempt to dilute the surrounding salt solution. This outward passage of water causes the cells to shrink and become wrinkled or crenated.

c. **Hypotonic:** if the blood is mixed with 0.2% NaCl solution or with distilled water, water enters the blood cells, causing them to swell and finally burst, with the liberation of hemoglobin.The salt solution in this instance is said to be with respect to the blood cell contents. Finally, This phenomenon is known ashemolysis .

Steps to Prepare Isotonic Solutions

Preparing isotonic solutions involves several steps to ensure that the final solution has the same osmotic pressure as body fluids, such as blood or tears, to avoid causing cell damage or discomfort when administered. Here are the detailed steps:

1. Determine the Desired Osmolarity

- **Target Osmolarity**: Typically, isotonic solutions have an osmolarity of around 290 mOsm/L, similar to that of body fluids.

- **Selection of Solute**: Common solutes used include sodium chloride (NaCl), dextrose, and other electrolytes.

2. Calculate the Required Amount of Solute

- **Molecular Weight**: Know the molecular weight of the solute(s) you are using.
- **Osmolarity Contribution**: Determine the contribution of each solute to the osmolarity of the solution. For NaCl, it dissociates into two ions (Na+ and Cl-), so each mole contributes twice the osmolarity.
- **Formula for Calculation**: Use the formula to calculate the mass of the solute required:

$$\text{Mass (g)} = \left(\frac{\text{Desired osmolarity (mOsm/L)} \times \text{Volume (L)} \times \text{Molecular weight (g}}{\text{Number of particles} \times 1000} \right.$$

3. Prepare the Solute

- **Weigh the Solute**: Accurately weigh the calculated amount of the solute using an analytical balance.
- **Dissolve in Solvent**: Dissolve the solute in a portion of the solvent, typically distilled or deionized water.

4. Adjust the Volume

- **Final Volume**: Transfer the solution to a volumetric flask and dilute to the final desired volume with distilled or deionized water.

5. Check Osmolarity

- **Osmometer**: Use an osmometer to measure the osmolarity of the solution and ensure it is isotonic. Adjust if necessary by adding more solute or diluting with solvent.

6. pH Adjustment (if necessary)

- **pH Measurement**: Measure the pH of the solution using a calibrated pH meter.

- **Adjust pH**: If necessary, adjust the pH by adding small amounts of acid (e.g., hydrochloric acid) or base (e.g., sodium hydroxide) to reach the desired pH.

7. Sterilization (if required)

- **Filtration**: Sterilize the solution by passing it through a 0.22-micron filter if it will be used for injection or other sterile applications.
- **Autoclaving**: Alternatively, autoclave the solution if the components are heat-stable.

8. Quality Control

- **Final Checks**: Recheck the osmolarity and pH of the solution to ensure they meet the specifications.
- **Documentation**: Record all measurements, adjustments, and observations during the preparation process.

9. Storage

- **Labeling**: Label the container with the contents, concentration, osmolarity, pH, date of preparation, and any other relevant information.
- **Storage Conditions**: Store the solution in appropriate conditions (e.g., temperature, light protection) to maintain its stability and sterility.

Example Preparation of Isotonic Sodium Chloride Solution (0.9% NaCl)

1. **Determine Desired Osmolarity**:
   - Target osmolarity: 290 mOsm/L (isotonic with body fluids).
2. **Calculate Required Amount of NaCl**:
   - Molecular weight of NaCl = 58.44 g/mol.
   - For a 1 L solution:

$$\text{Mass (g)} = \left(\frac{290 \times 1 \times 58.44}{2 \times 1000} \right) = 8.48 \text{ g}$$

Alternatively, for 0.9% NaCl solution, use 9 g NaCl per liter.

3. **Prepare the Solute**:
    - Weigh 9 g of NaCl.
    - Dissolve in approximately 800 mL of distilled water.
4. **Adjust the Volume**:
    - Transfer the solution to a 1 L volumetric flask and dilute to the 1 L mark with distilled water.
5. **Check Osmolarity**:
    - Measure the osmolarity using an osmometer.
    - Adjust if necessary.
6. **pH Adjustment (if necessary)**:
    - Measure pH and adjust if required.
7. **Sterilization (if required)**:
    - Filter sterilize or autoclave the solution.
8. **Quality Control**:
    - Recheck osmolarity and pH.
    - Document the preparation process.
9. **Storage**:
    - Label and store the solution under appropriate conditions.

GENERAL PRINCIPLES FOR ADJUSTMENT OF ISOTONICITY:

Adjusting the isotonicity of pharmaceutical solutions is crucial to ensure they match the osmotic pressure of body fluids, thus preventing irritation or damage to tissues. Here are the general principles for adjusting isotonicity:

1. Determine Desired Osmolarity

- **Target Osmolarity**: Aim for an osmolarity of approximately 290 mOsm/L, which is isotonic with body fluids such as blood and tears.

2. Identify the Active Ingredients

- **Calculate Contribution**: Determine the osmolarity contribution of active pharmaceutical ingredients (APIs) and other components in the solution.

3. Selection of Isotonicity Adjusting Agents

- **Common Agents**: Use agents such as sodium chloride (NaCl), dextrose, mannitol, or other electrolytes that are commonly used to adjust isotonicity.
- **Compatibility**: Ensure the selected agent is compatible with the APIs and other excipients in the formulation.

4. Calculation of Required Amounts

- **Freezing Point Depression Method**: This method is based on the principle that an isotonic solution has a freezing point depression of approximately -0.52°C. Calculate the amount of isotonicity-adjusting agent needed using the formula:

$$\Delta T_f = i \cdot K_f \cdot m$$

where ΔT_f is the freezing point depression, i is the van't Hoff factor (number of particles the solute dissociates into), K_f is the cryoscopic constant of the solvent (for water, 1.86°C·kg/mol), and m is the molality.

- **Sodium Chloride Equivalent Method (E Value)**: Calculate the amount of NaCl required to make the solution isotonic and adjust accordingly with the isotonicity-adjusting agent:

$$E \text{ Value} = \frac{\text{mass of solute}}{\text{mass of NaCl providing the same osmotic pressure}}$$

Calculate the amount of NaCl needed and use the E Value to determine the equivalent amount of the other isotonicity-adjusting agent.

5. Preparation and Adjustment

- **Dissolve Solutes**: Dissolve the calculated amounts of APIs and isotonicity-adjusting agents in a suitable volume of solvent (usually distilled or deionized water).
- **Measure Osmolarity**: Use an osmometer to measure the osmolarity of the solution.

- **Adjust Osmolarity**: If the osmolarity is not within the desired range, adjust by adding more isotonicity-adjusting agent or diluting the solution with solvent.

6. Verification and pH Adjustment

- **Osmolarity Check**: Recheck the osmolarity to confirm it is isotonic.
- **pH Adjustment**: Ensure the pH of the solution is within the acceptable range for the intended application. Adjust if necessary using pH-adjusting agents.

7. Sterilization and Final Preparation

- **Sterilization**: If required, sterilize the solution by filtration through a 0.22-micron filter or by autoclaving, provided the components are heat-stable.
- **Final Checks**: Perform final checks for osmolarity, pH, and sterility.

8. Documentation and Storage

- **Record-Keeping**: Document all calculations, measurements, adjustments, and observations during the preparation process.
- **Proper Storage**: Store the isotonic solution in appropriate, labeled containers under specified conditions to maintain stability and sterility.

Example: Adjusting Isotonicity of a Dextrose Solution

1. **Determine Desired Osmolarity**:
   - Target osmolarity: 290 mOsm/L.
2. **Identify Active Ingredients**:
   - Dextrose is the active ingredient.
3. **Selection of Isotonicity Adjusting Agent**:
   - Sodium chloride (NaCl) will be used for adjustment.
4. **Calculation of Required Amounts**:
   - Calculate the osmolarity contribution of dextrose.

- Use the sodium chloride equivalent (E Value) to determine additional NaCl needed: E Value of dextrose=0.18\text{E Value} \text{ of dextrose} = 0.18E Value of dextrose=0.18
- Calculate the amount of NaCl required to make the solution isotonic.

5. **Preparation and Adjustment**:
   - Dissolve dextrose in distilled water.
   - Add the calculated amount of NaCl.
   - Measure the osmolarity and adjust if necessary.

6. **Verification and pH Adjustment**:
   - Recheck osmolarity.
   - Adjust pH if required.

7. **Sterilization and Final Preparation**:
   - Sterilize the solution by filtration or autoclaving.

8. **Documentation and Storage**:
   - Document the preparation process.
   - Store the solution in labeled containers under appropriate conditions.

CALCULATIONS FOR SOLUTIONS ISOTONIC WITH BLOOD AND TEARS.:

1. Method based on freezing point data.
2. Method based on molecular concentration.
3. Graphic method based on vapour pressure and freezing- point depression.
4. Method based on sodium chloride equivalent.

1. METHOD BASED ON FREEZING POINT DATA:

- Physical properties of solutions- colligative properties.

   a) Osmotic pressure

   b) Depression of freezing point- simpler.

- Temperature at which blood plasma and tears freeze is -0.52^{0}C.

- Any solutions which freeze at –0.52^{0}C is isotonic with blood plasma and tears.

GENERAL FORMULA FOR CALCULATION FOR SOLUTIONS TO BE MADE ISO- OSMOTIC WITH BLOOD SERUM IS AS FOLLOWS:

Percentage W/V of adjusting substance needed = $\dfrac{0.52 - a}{b}$

Where a = Freezing point of the unadjusted solution

b= Freezing point of a 1% w/v solution of the adjusting substance.

2. METHOD BASED ON MOLECULAR CONCENTRATION:

- Molecular concentration: number of units i.e. molecules or ions or both present in a solution.

- A solution containing 1 g molecule of a non- ionising solute in 22.4 litres at normal temperature and pressure (NTP) has an atmospheric pressure of one atmosphere.

- Therefore a solution containing one gram molecule in 1 litre (a mole solution) will have osmotic pressure of 22.4 atmosphere.

- Osmotic pressure of blood plasma and lachrymal secretion is approximately 6.7 atmosphere.

Molarity of these fluids = 6.7/22.4 = 0.3 M (approx.)

Conc. of un- ionised medicaments needed to produce iso- osmotic solutions, W= 0.3 M

where W= concentration required in g per litre.

M= molecular weight of the solute.

In case of ionised medicaments, W= 0.3 M/ N

N= no. of ions

3. GRAPHIC METHOD BASED ON VAPOUR PRESSURE AND FREEZINGPOINT DEPRESSION.

- Solutions of various concentration of NaCl are prepared.
- Their freezing points are determined with accuracy.
- A graph is prepared from this data.
- Percentage concentration versus freezing point.
- Prepared for each medicament.
- Percentage of adjusting substances required to make any percentage of medicament isotonic with blood plasma can be determined.

4. METHOD BASED ON SODIUM CHLORIDE EQUIVALENT:

Factor called 'sodium chloride equivalent' which can be used to convert a specified concentration of medicament to the concentrate of sodium chloride which will produce same osmotic effect.

$$\text{Sodium chloride equivalant of a medicament} = \frac{\text{Freezing point depression produced by a solution of medicament}}{\text{Freezing point depression produced by NaCl solution of the same strength}}$$

PERCENTAGE CALCULATIONS:

1. Per cent w/w
2. Per cent w/v
3. Per cent v/v
4. Per cent v/w

COMMON FORMULAE USED IN PERCENTAGE CALCULATIONS:

$$\text{Strength of dilute solution} = \frac{\text{Strength of concentrate}}{\text{Degree of dilution}}$$

$$\text{Volume of stronger alcohol to be used} = \frac{\text{Volume required} \times \text{Percentage required}}{\text{Percentage used}}$$

$$\text{Weight of stronger alcohol to be used} = \frac{\text{Volume required} \times \text{Percentage required}}{\text{Percentage used}}$$

The formula for calculating the w/v percent of ionizing and non-ionizing substances required to make isotonic solutions with blood plasma is as follows;

1. For non-ionizing substances:

    W / V % of substance required = 0.03% x Gram molecular weight

2. For ionizing substances

    W/V % of substance required = 0.03% x Gram molecular weight / no. of ions yielded by the molecule

Question.1: Find the proportion of Boric Acid required to make a solution isotonic. The molecular weight of boric acid is 62, and it is a non-ionizing substance Solution:

- By applying formulae for non-ionizing substances;
- W/V % of boric acid required to make isotonic solution = 0.03% x gram molecular weight

$$= 0.03 \text{ x } 62 = 1.86$$

- So, 1.86 gms of boric acid is required to make 100ml isotonic solution.

Question.2: Find the proportion of Sodium sulphate required to make a solution isotonic. The molecular weight boric of sodium sulphate is 148, and it is an ionizing substance.

- By applying formulae for ionizing substances;
- W/V % of ionizing substance required to make isotonic solution = 0.03% x gram molecular weight / no. of ions

  $Na_2SO4 \longrightarrow 2Na + SO_4$

- So, total no. of ions produced by sodium sulphate = 3
- W/V % of Na2SO4 required to make isotonic solution = 0.03% x gram molecular weight / no. of ions

$$= 0.03 \% \times 148 / 3 = 1.48$$

- S0, 1.48 gm of sodium sulphate is required to make 100ml isotonic solution.

CHAPTER – 7

MAJOR EXTRA AND INTRACELLULAR ELECTROLYTES

Ms. Neha Goel

Associate Professor, Rajiv Gandhi Institute of Pharmacy, Faculty of Pharmaceutical Science & Technology, AKS University Satna, MP-India

ABSTRACT:

Electrolytes are essential minerals that carry an electric charge and are vital for numerous physiological functions in the body. Major extracellular electrolytes include sodium (Na^+), chloride (Cl^-), and bicarbonate (HCO_3^-). Sodium plays a crucial role in maintaining fluid balance, nerve function, and muscle contractions, while chloride helps in maintaining osmotic pressure and acid-base balance. Bicarbonate acts as a buffer to regulate pH levels in the blood. On the other hand, major intracellular electrolytes include potassium (K^+), magnesium (Mg^{2+}), and phosphate (HPO_4^{2-}). Potassium is vital for cell function, especially in nerve impulse transmission and muscle contraction. Magnesium is involved in over 300 biochemical reactions, including protein synthesis and muscle and nerve function. Phosphate is crucial for energy production, as it forms part of ATP, the energy currency of the cell. The balance of these electrolytes is tightly regulated by the body to ensure proper physiological function, with the kidneys playing a significant role in this regulation. Imbalances in electrolytes can lead to serious health issues, highlighting their importance in maintaining homeostasis.

Electrolyte: An electrolyte is any substance that dissociates into ions in aqueous solution. Ions can be positively charged (cations) or negatively charged (anions).

The major electrolytes found in the human body are:

- Sodium (Na+),

- Chloride (Cl^-)
- Potassium ($K+$),
- Phosphate ($HPO4^{--}$)
- Calcium ($Ca++$)
- Sulfate ($SO4^{--}$)
- Magnesium ($Mg++$)
- Bicarbonate ($HCO3^-$)

ELECTROLYTES IN BODY FLUID COMPARTMENTS:

- Intracellular: K, Mg, P
- Extracellular: Na, Cl, HCO3-

The electrolyte concentration will vary with a particular fluid compartment. The three compartments are:

1. Intracellular fluid (45-50% of body weight)

2. Interstitial fluid (12- 15% of body weight)

3. Plasma or vascular fluid (4-5% of body weight)

`   The term 'extracellular fluid' includes both interstitial and vascular fluids. These three compartments are separated from each other by membranes that are permeable to water and many organic and inorganic solutes

FUNCTIONS OF MAJOR PHYSIOLOGICAL IONS

A. Physiological role of sodium:

1. This plays a crucial role in the excitability of muscles and neurones.
2. It is also of crucial importance in regulating fluid balance in the body.
3. Sodium levels are extremely closely regulated by kidney function.
4. Sodium is easily filtered in the glomerular portion of the kidneys and most of it is reabsorbed in the kidney tubules.
5. Major factors that control the GFR include the blood pressure at the glomerulus and the stimulation of renal arteriole by the sympathetic nervous system.

6. The amount of sodium reabsorbed in the proximal convoluted tubule remains almost constantly at around 67%.

7. Sodium plays a key role in normal nerve and muscle function.

8. It is also a stimulator for aldosterone release from the adrenal glands. Because water has a close chemical affinity for sodium, it will follow that more water is reabsorbed in the kidney as well and this will put up the BP to a normal level.

9. An increase in the arterial BP will result in the release of atrial natriuretic factor (ANF) from the left and right atria of the heart.

10. This hormone actually inhibits renin and aldosterone release. By so doing the loss of sodium by the kidneys is enhanced by the decrease of aldosterone stimulated reabsorption.

11. As we have already seen that water will follow sodium, it follows that water is lost from the body allowing the BP to drop to a normal level.

B. Physiological role of potassium

1. Potassium is the major cation of intracellular fluid. Concentration within the cells is 28x that of the extra cellular fluids. As with sodium it is extremely important in the correct functioning of excitable cells such as muscles, neurons, sensory receptors etc.

2. It is also importantly involved in the regulation of fluid levels within the cell and in maintaining the correct pH balance within the body.

3. Potassium output is usually equal to potassium input. Sodium reabsorption by aldosterone is usually in exchange for either hydrogen ions or potassium ions. Therefore if sodium ions are reabsorbed more potassium is lost and vice versa. Thus, high levels of potassium in the interstitial fluid stimulate aldosterone response.

4. Diseases such as Cushing's disease (over production of ACTH) and hyperaldosteronism (overproduction of aldosterone) can lead to a

condition known as hypokalaemia (symptoms caused by low potassium levels) which manifests in muscle weakness, flaccid paralysis, cardiac arrhythmia and alkalosis.

5. The pH balance of the body also affects potassium levels. In acidosis potassium excretion is decreased (leads to hyperkalaemia higher than normal levels of potassium) whereas the opposite occurs in alkalosis.

C. **Physiological role of calcium**

1. Calcium is found mainly in the extracellular fluids whilst phosphorous is found mostly in the intracellular fluids. Both are important in the maintenance of healthy bone and teeth.

2. Calcium is also important in the transmission of nerve impulses across synapses, the clotting of blood and the contraction of muscles. If the levels of calcium fall below normal level both muscles and nerves become more excitable.

3. Calcium is an essential element that serves an important role in skeletal mineralization. More than 99% of the calcium in the body is stored in bone as hydroxyapatite.

4. Calcium in this form provides skeletal strength as well as a reservoir for calcium to be released into the serum.

D. **Physiological role of phosphate:**

1. Phosphate is required in the synthesis of nucleic acids and high-energy compounds such as ATP.

2. It is also important in the maintenance of pH balance

3. Phosphate is a charged particle (ion) that contains the mineral phosphorus.

4. The body needs phosphorus to build and repair bones and teeth, help nerves function, and make muscles contract. ... A hormone called

parathyroid hormone (PTH) regulates the levels of calcium and phosphorus in your blood.

E. **Physiological role of magnesium:**

1. Most magnesium is found in the intracellular fluid and in bone. Within cells, magnesium functions in the sodium-potassium pump and as an aid to the action of enzymes.
2. It plays a role in muscle contraction, action potential conduction, and bone and teeth production.
3. Magnesium is needed for more than 300 biochemical reactions in the body.
4. It helps to maintain normal nerve and muscle function, supports a healthy immune system, keeps the heartbeat steady, and helps bones remain strong.
5. It also helps adjust blood glucose levels. It aids in the production of energy and protein.
6. Aldosterone controls magnesium concentrations in the extracellular fluid. Low Mg^{++} levels result in an increased aldosterone secretion and the aldosterone increases Mg^{++} reabsorption by the kidneys.

F. **Physiological role of chloride:**

1. Chloride (Cl-) is the most plentiful extracellular anion with an extracellular concentration 26 times that of its intracellular concentration.
2. Chloride ions are able to diffuse easily across plasma membranes and their transport is closely linked to sodium movement, which also explains the indirect role of aldosterone in chlorine regulation.
3. When sodium is reabsorbed, chlorine follows passively. It helps to regulate osmotic pressure differences between fluid compartments and is essential in pH balance.

4. The chloride shift within the blood helps to move bicarbonate ions out of the red blood cells and into the plasma for transport. In the gastric mucosa, chlorine and hydrogen combine to form hydrochloric acid.

5. It also helps maintain proper blood volume, blood pressure, and pH of your body fluids.

G. Physiological role of bicarbonate:

1. Bicarbonate is alkaline and a vital component of the pH buffering system of the human body (maintaining acid-base homeostasis).

2. 70 to 75 percent of CO_2 in the body is converted into carbonic acid (H_2CO_3), which can quickly turn into bicarbonate (HCO^-).

3. With carbonic acid as the central intermediate species, bicarbonate – in conjunction with water, hydrogen ions, and carbon dioxide – forms this buffering system, which is maintained at the volatile equilibrium required to provide prompt resistance to drastic pH changes in both the acidic and basic directions.

4. This is especially important for protecting tissues of the central nervous system, where pH changes too far outside of the normal range in either direction could prove disastrous.

5. Bicarbonate also acts to regulate pH in the small intestine.

6. It is released from the pancreas in response to the hormone secretin to neutralize the acidic chyme entering the duodenum from the stomach

ELECTROLYTES USED IN THE REPLACEMENT THERAPY

Electrolyte replacement therapy is essential in medical practice to restore and maintain proper electrolyte balance in patients, particularly those experiencing imbalances due to illness, dehydration, or other medical conditions. The major electrolytes used in replacement therapy and their primary functions are as follows:

1. Sodium (Na^+)

- **Forms**: Sodium chloride (NaCl), sodium bicarbonate (NaHCO$_3$), sodium acetate (CH$_3$COONa).
- **Functions**:
  - Maintains fluid balance and osmotic pressure.
  - Essential for nerve impulse transmission and muscle function.
  - Regulates acid-base balance.
- **Usage**: Used to treat hyponatremia (low sodium levels) and in intravenous fluids to maintain hydration and electrolyte balance.

2. Potassium (K$^+$)

- **Forms**: Potassium chloride (KCl), potassium phosphate (K$_2$HPO$_4$), potassium acetate (CH$_3$COOK).
- **Functions**:
  - Maintains intracellular osmotic pressure.
  - Crucial for muscle contraction, including cardiac muscle.
  - Facilitates nerve impulse transmission.
  - Regulates acid-base balance.
- **Usage**: Used to treat hypokalemia (low potassium levels) and as a supplement in intravenous fluids to maintain electrolyte balance.

3. Calcium (Ca^{2+})

- **Forms**: Calcium gluconate, calcium chloride (CaCl$_2$), calcium lactate.
- **Functions**:
  - Essential for bone and teeth formation.
  - Necessary for blood coagulation.
  - Important for muscle contraction and nerve function.
- **Usage**: Used to treat hypocalcemia (low calcium levels), tetany, and as a supplement in parenteral nutrition.

4. Magnesium (Mg^{2+})

- **Forms**: Magnesium sulfate (MgSO$_4$), magnesium chloride (MgCl$_2$), magnesium oxide.

- **Functions**:
  - o Involved in over 300 enzymatic reactions, including ATP synthesis.
  - o Important for muscle relaxation and nerve function.
  - o Helps maintain normal muscle and nerve function.
- **Usage**: Used to treat hypomagnesemia (low magnesium levels), eclampsia, and as a supplement in parenteral nutrition.

5. Chloride (Cl^-)

- **Forms**: Sodium chloride ($NaCl$), potassium chloride (KCl).
- **Functions**:
  - o Maintains osmotic pressure and fluid balance.
  - o Essential component of gastric hydrochloric acid (HCl) for digestion.
  - o Helps maintain acid-base balance.
- **Usage**: Used in combination with sodium or potassium to maintain electrolyte balance in intravenous fluids.

6. Bicarbonate (HCO_3^-)

- **Forms**: Sodium bicarbonate ($NaHCO_3$).
- **Functions**:
  - o Primary buffer for maintaining acid-base balance in the blood.
  - o Helps neutralize excess acid in the body.
- **Usage**: Used to treat metabolic acidosis and to alkalinize urine.

7. Phosphate (PO_4^{3-})

- **Forms**: Potassium phosphate (K_2HPO_4), sodium phosphate (Na_2HPO_4).
- **Functions**:
  - o Essential for energy production (ATP).
  - o Important for bone and teeth formation.
  - o Acts as a buffer in maintaining acid-base balance.

- **Usage**: Used to treat hypophosphatemia (low phosphate levels) and as a supplement in parenteral nutrition.

8. Sulfate (SO_4^{2-})

- **Forms**: Magnesium sulfate ($MgSO_4$).
- **Functions**:
  - Helps in detoxification processes.
  - Component of proteins and enzymes.
- **Usage**: Used to treat magnesium deficiency and as an anticonvulsant in eclampsia.

Administration Routes

- **Oral**: Tablets, capsules, or oral solutions.
- **Intravenous (IV)**: Direct infusion into the bloodstream, often used in acute settings.

Monitoring and Safety

- **Regular Monitoring**: Blood levels of electrolytes should be regularly monitored to avoid imbalances and associated complications.
- **Dosage Adjustments**: Adjustments in dosage may be necessary based on patient response and electrolyte levels.
- **Patient Condition**: Consider the underlying health conditions, kidney function, and concurrent medications that may affect electrolyte balance.

SODIUM CHLORIDE

Synonym: Rock salt, Common Salt, Table salt

Physical Properties

- **Appearance**: White crystalline solid.
- **Solubility**: Highly soluble in water (359 g/L at 25°C), slightly soluble in ethanol.
- **Taste**: Salty.
- **Melting Point**: 801°C.

- **Boiling Point**: 1,413°C.
- **Density**: 2.165 g/cm³.
- **Crystal Structure**: Cubic.

Chemical Properties

- **Molecular Formula**: NaCl.
- **Molecular Weight**: 58.44 g/mol.
- **pH**: Neutral (around 7) when dissolved in water.
- **Ionic Compound**: Composed of sodium (Na^+) and chloride (Cl^-) ions.
- When react with silver nitrate it gives silver chloride.

$$NaCl + AgNO_3 \quad = \quad AgCl + NaNO_2$$

- When react with potassium permagnate it evolve chlorine gas.

- In its aqueous state NaCl acts as a good conductor of electricity due to the free movement of the ions.

- **Reactivity**:
  - Reacts with sulfuric acid to produce hydrochloric acid (HCl) and sodium sulfate (Na_2SO_4).
  - Reacts with silver nitrate ($AgNO_3$) to form a white precipitate of silver chloride (AgCl).

Preparation

- **Natural Sources**:
  - **Mining**: Extracted from rock salt deposits (halite).
  - **Evaporation**: Obtained by evaporating seawater or brine from salt lakes.
- **Industrial Preparation**:

- o **Electrolysis of Brine**: Produces sodium hydroxide (NaOH), chlorine gas (Cl_2), and hydrogen gas (H_2). Sodium chloride is left behind as a byproduct.

Tests

- **Qualitative Tests**:
  - o **Flame Test**: Sodium ions impart a bright yellow color to a flame.
  - o **Silver Nitrate Test**: A solution of sodium chloride reacts with silver nitrate to form a white precipitate of silver chloride (AgCl). NaCl+AgNO3→AgCl↓+NaNO3\text{NaCl} + \text{AgNO}_3 \rightarrow \text{AgCl} \downarrow + \text{NaNO}_3NaCl+AgNO3→AgCl↓+NaNO3
- **Quantitative Tests**:
  - o **Gravimetric Analysis**: Determination of chloride by precipitating as silver chloride and weighing.
  - o **Titrimetric Analysis**: Titration with a silver nitrate solution using potassium chromate as an indicator (Mohr's method).

Chemical reaction:

1. When react with silver nitrate it gives silver chloride.

$$NaCl + AgNO_3 \;=\; AgCl + NaNO_2$$

2. When react with potassium permagnate it evolve chlorine gas.

3. In its aqueous state NaCl acts as a good conductor of electricity due to the free movement of the ions.

Preparation:

1. 1 mol of sodium bicarbonate reacts with 1 mol of hydrochloric acid to generate 1 mol of salt, 1 mol of water, and/or 1 mol of carbon dioxide.

$$NaOH + HCl = NaCl + H2O$$

Assay:

Principle: The assay of sodium chloride is dependent on the modified Volhard's method in which indirect volumetric precipitation titration is involved. An acidified solution of sodium chloride with nitric acid is treated with a measured excess amount of standard solution of silver nitrate in the presence of nitrobenzene. Some of the silver nitrate is consumed in the reaction with sodium chloride. The remaining unreacted $AgNO_3$ is determined by titration with standard solution of ammonium thiocyanate using ferric alum (ferric ammonium sulphate) as indicator. The end point is obtained as a permanent brick red color due to formation of ferric thiocyanate.

Procedure: Accurately weigh the substance (0.1 gm) and dissolve in 50 ml water. Add 50 ml of 0.1N $AgNO_3$, 3 ml HNO_3, 5 ml nitro benzene, 2 ml ferric ammonium sulphate and mix thoroughly. The solution is titrated with ammonium thiocyanate until the color becomes brick red. 1ml of 0.1N $AgNO_3$ $\equiv 0.005844$ gm NaCl

Uses

- Medical **Uses:**
    - **IV Fluids**: Sodium chloride solutions (0.9% w/v) are used for intravenous hydration and electrolyte balance (normal saline).
    - **Oral Rehydration**: Component of oral rehydration salts (ORS) for treating dehydration.
    - **Wound Care**: Used as a saline solution for wound irrigation and cleaning.
- **Industrial Uses:**
    - **Food Industry**: Used as a preservative and flavor enhancer (table salt).

- **Chemical Industry**: Used in the manufacture of various chemicals including sodium hydroxide, chlorine, and hydrogen chloride.
- **Laboratory Uses**:
  - **Reagent**: Common reagent in analytical chemistry for titrations and standardizations.
  - **Buffer Preparation**: Used in the preparation of buffer solutions.

Official Preparations

- Pharmacopoeial Standards: Sodium chloride is listed in various pharmacopoeias, including the United States Pharmacopeia (USP) and the British Pharmacopoeia (BP), with standards for purity, preparation, and usage.
- **Formulations**:
  - **Normal Saline (0.9% NaCl)**: Used for intravenous infusion, irrigation, and diluent for medications.
  - **Hypertonic Saline (3% or 5% NaCl)**: Used in certain medical conditions requiring a higher concentration of sodium.
  - **Sodium Chloride Injection**: Sterile solution for intravenous administration.
  - **Sodium Chloride Tablets**: Used to replenish sodium levels in patients with hyponatremia or salt-losing conditions.
  - **Sodium Chloride Ophthalmic Solution**: Used for relief of eye dryness and irritation.
  - **Sodium Chloride Nasal Spray**: Used to moisturize nasal passages and alleviate nasal congestion.

Preparation of Normal Saline (0.9% NaCl Solution)

1. **Materials Needed**:

- o Sodium chloride (NaCl), USP grade.
- o Distilled or sterile water.
- o Volumetric flask.
- o Analytical balance.

2. **Procedure**:

- o Weigh 9 grams of sodium chloride.
- o Dissolve the sodium chloride in approximately 800 mL of distilled water.
- o Transfer the solution to a 1-liter volumetric flask.
- o Add distilled water to bring the final volume to 1 liter.
- o Mix thoroughly until the sodium chloride is completely dissolved.
- o Sterilize the solution if necessary, using filtration or autoclaving.

Official preparation of sodium chloride:

1. Sodium chloride injection I.P
2. Sodium chloride hypertonic injection I.P
3. Compound Sodium chloride injection I.P
4. Bacteriostatic Sodium chloride injection I.P
5. Sodium chloride & Dextrose injection I.P
6. Sodium chloride & Mannitol injection I.P
7. Sodium chloride tablets I.P
8. Compound Sodium chloride & dextrose oral powderI .P
9. Sodium chloride eye lotion B.P
10. Sodium chloride solution B.P

Sodium chloride Injection I.P:

- It is sterile isotonic solution of NaCl in water for injection.

- I.P.- 0.85-0.95% w/v (150 milimoles of sodium chloride ions per litre)

- B.P.- 95-105% w/v

- When it is required as diluent for other Pharmacopoeial injctions, 0.9% w/v solution of NaCl is used.

Sodium chloride Hypertonic Injection I.P:

- It is sterile isotonic solution of NaCl in water for injection contain not less than 1. 52% and not more than 1.68% w/v of sodium chloride.
- (270 milimoles of sodium chloride ions per litre)
- no antimicrobial ions are present.

Compound Sodium Chloride Injection I.P. (Ringer injection):

- It contains not less than 0.82 % and not more than 0.9 % w/v of sodium chloride, not less than 0.0285 %, not more than 0.0315 % w/v of potassium chloride and not less than 0.03 % and not more than 0.036% w/v of calcium chloride in water for injection.
- It contains no antimicrobial agents.
- It is a clear, colorless solution with pH between 5-7.5
- Sodium chloride eye lotion B.P

    0.85-0.95% w/v of NaCl

- Sodium chloride solution B.P

    - 0.9% w/v solution

- Normal saline solution

    If sterile- it is completely free from micro organisms.

Sodium Chloride Tablets I.P

- 95-105% w/v of stated amount
- Strength available- 180,300,500mg

POTASSIUM CHLORIDE

Mol.formula: KCl   Molecular weight- 74.55

Synonym- potassium muriate, potash muriate

Physical Properties

- **Appearance**: White or colorless crystalline solid.

- **Solubility**: Highly soluble in water (344 g/L at 20°C), slightly soluble in ethanol.
- **Taste**: Salty, with a slightly bitter aftertaste.
- **Melting Point**: 770°C.
- **Boiling Point**: 1,420°C.
- **Density**: 1.984 g/cm³.
- **Crystal Structure**: Cubic.

Chemical Properties

- **Molecular Formula**: KCl.
- **Molecular Weight**: 74.55 g/mol.
- **pH**: Neutral (around 7) when dissolved in water.
- **Ionic Compound**: Composed of potassium (K^+) and chloride (Cl^-) ions.
- **Reactivity**:
    - Stable under normal conditions.
    - Reacts with concentrated sulfuric acid to produce hydrogen chloride (HCl) gas and potassium sulfate (K_2SO_4).

Preparation

- **Natural Sources**:
    - **Mining**: Extracted from mineral deposits such as sylvite and carnallite.
    - **Evaporation**: Obtained by evaporating brine solutions from salt lakes and seawater.
- Method 1: Potassium chloride can be prepared by treating potassium hydroxide (KOH) or other potassium bases (potassium carbonate, potassium sulphate) with hydrochloric acid:

$$KOH + HCl \rightarrow KCl + H_2O$$

This conversion is an acid-base neutralization reaction.

The resulting salt can then be purified by recrystallization.

- Method 2:

By allowing potassium to burn in the presence of chlorine gas (exothermic reaction)

$$2\,K + Cl_2 \rightarrow 2\,KCl$$

- **Industrial Preparation**:
  - **Electrolysis of Potassium Chloride**: Involved in the production of potassium hydroxide (KOH) and chlorine gas (Cl_2).

Storage

- **Conditions**:
  - Store in a tightly closed container to prevent moisture absorption.
  - Keep in a cool, dry place away from incompatible substances such as strong acids.
- **Packaging**: Often stored in plastic or glass containers, depending on the quantity and use.

Tests

- **Qualitative Tests**:
  - **Flame Test**: Potassium ions impart a lilac or light purple color to a flame.
  - **Silver Nitrate Test**: A solution of potassium chloride reacts with silver nitrate to form a white precipitate of silver chloride (AgCl).

    $$KCl + AgNO_3 \rightarrow AgCl\downarrow + KNO_3$$
- **Quantitative Tests**:
  - **Gravimetric Analysis**: Determination of chloride by precipitating as silver chloride and weighing.

- o **Titrimetric Analysis**: Titration with a silver nitrate solution using potassium chromate as an indicator (Mohr's method).

Uses

- **Medical Uses**:
  - o **Electrolyte Replacement**: Used to treat hypokalemia (low potassium levels) and in intravenous fluids to maintain electrolyte balance.
  - o **Oral Supplements**: Tablets and solutions for oral administration to prevent or treat potassium deficiency.
  - o **Cardioplegia**: Used in cardiac surgery to induce cardiac arrest during heart surgeries.
- **Industrial Uses**:
  - o **Fertilizers**: Major component of potash fertilizers due to its potassium content, essential for plant growth.
  - o **Food Industry**: Used as a salt substitute and preservative.
- **Laboratory Uses**:
  - o **Buffer Preparation**: Used in the preparation of various buffer solutions.
  - o **Standard Solutions**: Used to prepare standard solutions for calibration and analytical purposes.

Official Preparations

- **Pharmacopoeial Standards**: Listed in various pharmacopoeias, including the United States Pharmacopeia (USP) and the British Pharmacopoeia (BP), with standards for purity, preparation, and usage.
- **Formulations**:

- o **Potassium Chloride Injection**: Sterile solution for intravenous administration to correct electrolyte imbalances.
- o **Potassium Chloride Oral Solution**: Liquid form for oral intake to prevent or treat potassium deficiency.
- o **Potassium Chloride Tablets**: Solid dosage form for oral administration.
- o **Extended-Release Tablets**: Formulated for slow release of potassium to maintain levels over an extended period.

Preparation of Potassium Chloride Solution (for Intravenous Use)

1. **Materials Needed**:
   - o Potassium chloride (KCl), USP grade.
   - o Distilled or sterile water.
   - o Volumetric flask.
   - o Analytical balance.
2. **Procedure**:
   - o Weigh the required amount of potassium chloride (e.g., 7.45 g for a 100 mL of 10% w/v solution).
   - o Dissolve the potassium chloride in a portion of distilled water.
   - o Transfer the solution to a volumetric flask and dilute to the final desired volume with distilled water.
   - o Mix thoroughly until the potassium chloride is completely dissolved.
   - o Sterilize the solution if necessary, using filtration or autoclaving.

Official Preparation of Potassium chloride:

- Potassium chloride injection I.P
- Potassium chloride oral solution I.P
- Potassium chloride elixirs I.P
- Lactated Potassium chloride saline injection NF

- Potassium chloride & Sodium chloride I.V
- Infusion I.P
- Potassium chloride & Dextrose I.V infusion I.P
- Potassium chloride & Glucose I.V infusion I.P
- Potassium chloride tablets I.P

CALCIUM GLUCONATE

Mol. Formula: $C_{12}H_{22}CaO_{14}.H_2O$ **Mol. Wt.:** 430.37

Physical Properties:

- **Appearance**: White to off-white crystalline or granular powder.
- **Molecular Weight**: 430.37 g/mol (anhydrous form).
- **Melting Point**: Decomposes at about 120 °C (248 °F).
- **Solubility**: Sparingly soluble in water (3.5 g/L at 25 °C); practically insoluble in ethanol and other organic solvents.
- **Odor and Taste**: Odorless with a slightly bitter taste.

Preparation: Calcium gluconate can be synthesized through the neutralization of gluconic acid with calcium carbonate or calcium hydroxide. The process involves the following steps:

1. **Gluconic Acid Production**: Gluconic acid is produced by the oxidation of glucose using enzymes or microorganisms.
2. **Neutralization**: Gluconic acid is then neutralized with calcium carbonate ($CaCO_3$) or calcium hydroxide ($Ca(OH)_2$) to form calcium gluconate.

$$2C6H_{11}O_7H + CaCO_3 \rightarrow (C_6H_{11}O_7)_2Ca + CO_2 + H_2O$$

or

$$2C6H_{11}O_7H + Ca(OH)2 \rightarrow (C_6H_{11}O_7)_2Ca + 2H_2O$$

3. **Purification**: The resulting calcium gluconate solution is filtered and concentrated, and the product is then crystallized and dried.

Chemical Properties:

- **Chemical Formula**: $C_{12}H_{22}CaO_{14}$ (anhydrous form).

- **Stability**: Chemically stable under normal conditions.
- **Reactivity**: Calcium gluconate is relatively non-reactive but can form complexes with various anions.

Storage:

- **Conditions**: Store in a tightly closed container in a cool, dry place away from direct sunlight and moisture.
- **Precautions**: Avoid exposure to air and excessive heat. Proper storage conditions are essential to maintain its stability and prevent degradation.

Uses:

- **Medical**:
  - **Hypocalcemia Treatment**: Used to treat low blood calcium levels (hypocalcemia). It can be administered orally or intravenously.
  - **Antidote for Hyperkalemia and Magnesium Toxicity**: Administered intravenously to counteract the effects of elevated potassium or magnesium levels.
  - **Calcium Supplement**: Often included in dietary supplements to ensure adequate calcium intake.
  - **Bone Health**: Supports bone formation and maintenance, especially in conditions like osteoporosis.
- **Food Industry**: Used as a firming agent in food processing, particularly in canned vegetables and fruit products.
- **Laboratory**: Employed in various biochemical assays and as a reagent in laboratory settings.

Example Official Preparation: Calcium Gluconate Injection USP

- **Concentration**: Typically 10% (100 mg/mL of calcium gluconate).
- **Formulation**: Sterile, non-pyrogenic solution for intravenous administration.
- **Usage**: Prescribed for the treatment of hypocalcemia, hyperkalemia, and magnesium sulfate overdose.

Storage of Official Preparations:

- **Injection**: Store at controlled room temperature (20-25 °C or 68-77 °F). Protect from freezing and light.
- **Oral Tablets/Syrup**: Store at room temperature in a tightly closed container, away from moisture and heat.

Official preparation:

1. Calcium Gluconate
2. Calcium Gluconate injection
3. Calcium Gluconate Tablets

ORAL REHYDRATION SALT (ORS)

Oral Rehydration Salt (ORS) is a life-saving solution used to prevent and treat dehydration, especially due to diarrhea, vomiting, or other illnesses that cause significant fluid loss. ORS is a carefully balanced mixture of salts, sugars, and water that facilitates the quick and efficient absorption of fluids and electrolytes into the bloodstream. The World Health Organization (WHO) has developed a standard ORS formula that typically includes sodium chloride, potassium chloride, sodium citrate, and glucose. The glucose in ORS enhances the absorption of sodium and water in the intestines through the sodium-glucose co-transport mechanism.

ORS is particularly critical in areas with limited access to medical care, as it can be administered easily and effectively at home or in community health settings. The preparation of ORS involves dissolving the ORS powder in a specific amount of clean water, usually one liter, to ensure the correct concentration of electrolytes. This solution helps to restore the body's electrolyte balance and rehydrate tissues, preventing complications associated with severe dehydration, such as shock and organ failure.

The use of ORS is a cornerstone of global health strategies aimed at reducing mortality and morbidity associated with dehydration, particularly in children under five. It is cost-effective, easy to distribute, and has been shown to significantly reduce the incidence of dehydration-related deaths worldwide. Proper education on the preparation and use of ORS is essential for maximizing its benefits and ensuring its effectiveness in treating dehydration in various populations.

The old formula:

- Sodium Chloride 3.5 g
- Potassium Chloride 1.5 g
- Trisodium Citrate, dihydrate 2.9 g
- Glucose Anhydrous 20.0 g

New formula of ORH:

Reduced osmolarity ORS	grams /litre	Reduced osmolarity ORS	mmol/ litre
Sodium chloride	2.6	Sodium	75
Glucose, anhydrous	13.5	Chloride	65
Potassium chloride	1.5	Glucose, anhydrous	75
Trisodium citrate dihydrate	2.9	Potassium	20
		Citrate	10
Total weight	**20.5**	Total Osmolarity	**245**

PHYSIOLOGICAL ACID BASE BALANCE

Physiological acid-base balance is a critical aspect of homeostasis, ensuring that the body's internal environment remains within a narrow pH range, typically between 7.35 and 7.45. This balance is essential for the proper functioning of enzymes, metabolic processes, and cellular activities. The body employs several mechanisms to maintain this balance, including buffer systems, respiratory regulation, and renal regulation.

Buffer Systems

1. **Bicarbonate Buffer System**: The primary buffer system in the blood, consisting of bicarbonate (HCO_3^-) and carbonic acid (H_2CO_3). It helps neutralize excess acids or bases to stabilize pH.

$$H_2CO_3 \rightleftharpoons H^+ + HCO_3^-$$

Phosphate Buffer System: Operates mainly in the intracellular fluid and renal tubules. It involves dihydrogen phosphate ($H_2PO_4^-$) and hydrogen phosphate (HPO_4^{2-}).

$$H_2PO_4^- \rightleftharpoons H^+ + HPO_4^{2-}$$

2. **Protein Buffer System**: Proteins, particularly hemoglobin in red blood cells, act as buffers by binding to or releasing hydrogen ions (H^+).

Respiratory Regulation

The respiratory system controls the pH of body fluids by regulating the concentration of carbon dioxide (CO_2) in the blood. CO_2 combines with water to form carbonic acid, which dissociates into hydrogen ions and bicarbonate:

$$CO_2 + H_2O \rightleftharpoons H_2CO_3 \rightleftharpoons H^+ + HCO_3^-$$

By altering the rate and depth of breathing, the respiratory system can increase or decrease the elimination of CO_2, thereby adjusting the pH. Hyperventilation reduces CO_2 levels, raising pH (alkalosis), while hypoventilation increases CO_2 levels, lowering pH (acidosis).

Renal Regulation

The kidneys contribute to long-term acid-base balance by excreting or conserving hydrogen ions and bicarbonate. They achieve this through:

1. **Reabsorption of Bicarbonate**: The kidneys filter bicarbonate from the blood and reabsorb it back into the bloodstream, reducing acidity.

2. **Excretion of Hydrogen Ions**: The kidneys secrete hydrogen ions into the urine, which can combine with buffers like phosphate and ammonia to be excreted as salts.
3. **Generation of New Bicarbonate**: In the process of excreting hydrogen ions, the kidneys also generate new bicarbonate ions, which are added to the blood.

Disorders of Acid-Base Balance

1. **Acidosis**: Occurs when the pH falls below 7.35. It can be:
   - **Respiratory Acidosis**: Due to reduced CO_2 elimination (e.g., in lung diseases).
   - **Metabolic Acidosis**: Due to excess acid production or bicarbonate loss (e.g., in diabetic ketoacidosis, renal failure).
2. **Alkalosis**: Occurs when the pH rises above 7.45. It can be:
   - **Respiratory Alkalosis**: Due to increased CO_2 elimination (e.g., in hyperventilation).
   - **Metabolic Alkalosis**: Due to excessive bicarbonate retention or acid loss (e.g., in vomiting, diuretic use).

Maintaining acid-base balance is a complex, tightly regulated process involving the coordinated actions of the lungs, kidneys, and buffer systems. Disruptions in this balance can lead to significant health issues, requiring prompt medical intervention to restore homeostasis.

CHAPTER – 8

DENTAL PRODUCTS

Mrs. Priya Diwedi

Assistant Professor, Rajiv Gandhi Institute of Pharmacy, Faculty of

Pharmaceutical Science & Technology, AKS University Satna, MP-India

ABSTRACT:

Dental products play a crucial role in maintaining oral hygiene and preventing dental diseases such as cavities, gingivitis, and periodontal disease. These products include toothpaste, mouthwash, dental floss, interdental brushes, and dental sealants. Toothpaste is formulated with fluoride to strengthen enamel and prevent tooth decay, along with abrasive agents to remove plaque and stains. Mouthwash can contain antiseptics to reduce oral bacteria, as well as fluoride for additional protection. Dental floss and interdental brushes are essential for cleaning between teeth where toothbrush bristles cannot reach, effectively removing food particles and plaque. Dental sealants, typically applied by dentists, provide a protective coating on the chewing surfaces of back teeth to prevent decay. Advanced dental products also include whitening agents, such as peroxide-based gels, which help in removing surface stains and whitening teeth. In addition to these, products like denture cleaners and adhesives are vital for individuals with dentures, ensuring they remain clean, secure, and comfortable. The development of dental products continues to evolve with innovations like electric toothbrushes, which offer superior plaque removal through oscillating or sonic technology. Additionally, products infused with natural ingredients, such as charcoal or herbal extracts, cater to consumers seeking more natural oral care options. Proper use of these dental products, combined with regular dental check-ups, forms the cornerstone of effective oral health management, contributing to overall well-being and quality of life.

The substances used to produce effect on teeth and in dental cavity is called as dental product. E.g. Sodium fluoride

Dental hygiene is the most important for human body. There are many products are present in the market for the dental hygiene of the teeth and are considered as dental products.

Dental caries: Dental caries is a disease of teeth cause by acids produced by the action of microorganisms on carbohydrates so to prevent dental caries anticaries agents are used. Agents those used to prevent the tooth decay (caries).

Dentifrices: Dentifrices is a material which is used for cleaning of teeth and adjacent gums. Dentrifrices are applied as powders or pastes. Mainly phosphate is used in dentrifrices as a cleaning agent. Dentifrices are preparations meant to clean the teeth and other parts of oral cavity (gums) using a finger or a toothbrush. They are available as tooth powder, toothpastes, gels, dental creams and even as dental foams. They are meant to enhance the personal appearance of the teeth (daily removal of pellicles) by maintaining cleaner teeth, reduction of bad odor (removal of putrifying food particles from spaces between teeth) and also make the gum healthy

Desentisizing agents: Desentisizing agents are used in tooth decay or in perception of heat and cold. It is used to reduce sensitivity of heat and cold. It probably acts like local anesthetic. Desensitizing agents reduce sensitivity may be by acting as local anesthetics.

Cements and Fillers:

- Dental cements are used to temporarily cover protection that had gone operation
- It is applied as a paste which solidify later
- Eugenol is antiseptic and act as local anesthetic is used in cement as a medicated product
- Gold and silver are used as permanent filling

FLUORIDES

Fluorides are compounds that contain the element fluorine, which plays a crucial role in dental health by preventing tooth decay and strengthening tooth enamel. Fluoride works by enhancing the remineralization process, where minerals are redeposited in the enamel after being removed by acids from bacteria in the mouth. It also inhibits the demineralization process, reducing the solubility of tooth enamel in acid and thereby making teeth more resistant to decay.

Sources of Fluoride:

1. **Water Fluoridation**: One of the most effective public health measures for preventing dental caries is the addition of fluoride to public water supplies. This ensures that people receive a constant, low-level supply of fluoride.

2. **Toothpaste**: Most toothpastes contain fluoride, typically in the form of sodium fluoride (NaF) or stannous fluoride (SnF_2). Regular use helps to maintain fluoride levels on the tooth surface.

3. **Mouth Rinses**: Fluoride mouth rinses can provide additional protection for those at high risk of cavities. They are especially useful for children and individuals with orthodontic appliances.

4. **Professional Treatments**: Dentists can apply high-concentration fluoride treatments in the form of gels, foams, or varnishes during routine check-ups to give an extra layer of protection.

Preparation and Chemical Properties:

- **Chemical Formula**: Fluorides can vary; common examples include sodium fluoride (NaF), stannous fluoride (SnF_2), and sodium monofluorophosphate (Na_2PO_3F).

- **Stability**: These compounds are generally stable and effective at low concentrations.

- **Solubility**: Fluorides are typically soluble in water, which facilitates their use in dental products and water fluoridation.

Storage:

- **Conditions**: Store fluoride compounds in a cool, dry place, away from direct sunlight and moisture. Proper sealing of containers is important to prevent contamination and maintain efficacy.

Uses:

- **Cavity Prevention**: The primary use of fluoride is in the prevention of dental cavities. It is effective for both children and adults in reducing the incidence of caries.
- **Strengthening Enamel**: By promoting the remineralization of enamel, fluoride helps to make teeth more resistant to acid attacks from bacteria.
- **Treatment of Early Decay**: Fluoride can reverse early stages of tooth decay by facilitating the remineralization of weakened enamel.

TYPES OF DENTAL PRODUCT:

1. **Anti caries agent :** Sodium fluoride

2. **Cleaning agent /Dentrifices:** Dibasic calcium phosphate

3. **Polishing agent:** sodium metaphosphate

4. **Desensitization agents:** Zinc chloride

SODIUM FLUORIDE

Mol. Formula: NaF   **Mol.Wt:** 41.99

Physical Properties:

- **Appearance**: White, odorless crystalline powder or granules.
- **Molecular Weight**: 41.99 g/mol.
- **Melting Point**: 993 °C (1,819 °F).
- **Boiling Point**: 1,704 °C (3,099 °F).
- **Solubility**: Soluble in water (4 g/100 mL at 25 °C), slightly soluble in alcohol.
- **Taste**: Slightly saline and bitter taste.

Preparation: Sodium fluoride can be prepared by neutralizing hydrofluoric acid (HF) with sodium hydroxide (NaOH) or sodium carbonate (Na_2CO_3):

1. **Neutralization with Sodium Hydroxide:**

   $HF + NaOH \rightarrow NaF + H_2O$

2. **Neutralization with Sodium Carbonate:**

   $2HF + Na_2CO_3 \rightarrow 2NaF + H_2O + CO_2$

   The resulting sodium fluoride is then purified and dried to obtain the final product.

Chemical Properties:

- **Chemical Formula**: NaF.
- **Reactivity**: Sodium fluoride is a strong ionic compound and dissociates completely in water to form fluoride ions (F^-) and sodium ions (Na^+).
- **Stability**: Chemically stable under normal conditions but can react with acids to release hydrofluoric acid (HF).

Storage:

- **Conditions**: Store in a tightly closed container in a cool, dry place, away from incompatible substances such as strong acids and oxidizing agents.
- **Precautions**: Avoid exposure to moisture and air. Proper handling and storage conditions are essential to maintain its stability and effectiveness.

Uses:

- **Dental Care:**
  - **Toothpaste**: Commonly added to toothpaste to help prevent dental cavities by promoting remineralization of enamel and inhibiting the growth of harmful bacteria.
  - **Mouth Rinses**: Included in some mouth rinses to provide additional fluoride exposure.
  - **Professional Treatments**: Applied by dentists in the form of gels, foams, or varnishes for patients at high risk of dental caries.

- **Water Fluoridation**: Used in small quantities to fluoridate drinking water, helping to reduce the incidence of tooth decay in the population.
- **Industrial Applications**: Employed in the manufacturing of glass, ceramics, and for metallurgical processes.

Official Preparation: Sodium Fluoride Tablets USP

- **Formulation**: Tablets typically contain 0.5 mg, 1 mg, or 2.2 mg of sodium fluoride.
- **Usage**: Prescribed to prevent dental cavities, especially in areas where water fluoridation is not available or insufficient. The tablets can be chewed or dissolved in water before ingestion.
- **Administration**: Usually taken once daily, preferably at bedtime, after brushing the teeth.

Storage of Official Preparations:

- **Tablets**: Store at room temperature in a tightly closed container, away from moisture and heat.
- **Gels/Foams/Varnishes**: Store as per the manufacturer's instructions, typically at room temperature, and protect from light and moisture.

STANNOUS FLUORIDE

Mol. Formula: SnF_2 **Mol. Wt:** 156.70

Physical Properties:

- **Appearance**: White to off-white crystalline powder.
- **Molecular Weight**: 156.69 g/mol.
- **Melting Point**: 215 °C (419 °F).
- **Solubility**: Moderately soluble in water (25 g/L at 25 °C); slightly soluble in ethanol.
- **Odor and Taste**: Odorless with a slightly metallic taste.

Preparation: Stannous fluoride is typically prepared by reacting stannous oxide (SnO) or stannous chloride ($SnCl_2$) with hydrofluoric acid (HF):

1. **From Stannous Oxide:**

$$SnO + 2HF \rightarrow SnF_2 + H_2O$$

2. **From Stannous Chloride**:

$$SnCl2 + 2HF \rightarrow SnF_2 + 2HCl$$

The resultant stannous fluoride is then purified and dried to obtain the final product.

Chemical Properties:

- **Chemical Formula**: SnF_2.
- **Reactivity**: Stannous fluoride is a strong ionic compound that dissociates in water to release tin(II) ions (Sn^{2+}) and fluoride ions (F^-).
- **Stability**: It is stable under normal conditions but can hydrolyze in the presence of water to form hydrofluoric acid and tin hydroxide, especially at higher temperatures.

Storage:

- **Conditions**: Store in a tightly closed container in a cool, dry place, away from moisture, acids, and oxidizing agents.
- **Precautions**: Protect from exposure to air and moisture to prevent hydrolysis. Use appropriate personal protective equipment (PPE) when handling.

Uses:

- **Dental Care**:
    - **Toothpaste**: Widely used in fluoride toothpaste to prevent dental caries. Stannous fluoride provides both anticaries and antibacterial benefits.
    - **Mouth Rinses**: Included in some mouth rinses for additional protection against tooth decay and plaque formation.
    - **Professional Treatments**: Applied by dentists in various forms for patients with a high risk of dental caries.
- **Oral Hygiene**: Helps reduce tooth sensitivity by forming a protective barrier over exposed dentin and decreasing plaque formation.

- **Other Applications**: Used in some antiseptic and anti-inflammatory formulations.

Official Preparation: Stannous Fluoride Toothpaste USP

- **Formulation**: Typically contains 0.4% stannous fluoride, which is equivalent to 1,000 ppm of fluoride ions.
- **Usage**: Recommended for brushing teeth twice daily to prevent cavities and reduce tooth sensitivity.
- **Administration**: Apply a pea-sized amount of toothpaste to a toothbrush and brush thoroughly for at least two minutes. Rinse with water after brushing.

Storage of Official Preparations:

- **Toothpaste**: Store at room temperature, away from moisture and heat. Ensure the cap is tightly closed after each use to prevent the toothpaste from drying out and losing its efficacy.
- **Mouth Rinses**: Store at room temperature in a tightly sealed container, away from light and moisture.

CALCIUM CARBONATE

Mol. Formula: $CaCO_3$ **Mol. Wt:** 100.09

Synonyms: Precipitated Chalk, Calcii carbonas

Physical Properties:

- **Appearance**: White, odorless powder or crystalline solid.
- **Molecular Weight**: 100.09 g/mol.
- **Melting Point**: Decomposes at about 825 °C (1,517 °F) to calcium oxide (CaO) and carbon dioxide (CO_2).
- **Solubility**: Practically insoluble in water (0.013 g/L at 25 °C); soluble in acids with effervescence.
- **Density**: Approximately 2.71 g/cm³ (varies with polymorphic form).

Preparation: Calcium carbonate can be prepared through several methods, including:

1. **Mining and Processing**: Naturally occurring calcium carbonate is mined from quarries as limestone or marble. It is then ground and processed into a fine powder.

2. **Chemical Precipitation**: Calcium carbonate can be produced by the reaction of calcium hydroxide ($Ca(OH)_2$) with carbon dioxide (CO_2):
$Ca(OH)2+CO2 \rightarrow CaCO3+H2O$

3. **Reaction of Calcium Chloride with Sodium Carbonate**: Another method involves reacting calcium chloride ($CaCl_2$) with sodium carbonate (Na_2CO_3): $CaCl_2+Na_2CO_3 \rightarrow CaCO_3+2NaCl$

Chemical Properties:

- **Chemical Formula**: $CaCO_3$.
- **Stability**: Chemically stable under normal conditions.
- **Reactivity**: Reacts with acids to produce calcium salts, water, and carbon dioxide gas: $CaCO_3+2HCl \rightarrow CaCl2+H_2O+CO_2$

  Decomposes on heating to form calcium oxide and carbon dioxide:
$$CaCO_3 \rightarrow CaO+CO_2 \text{ (at } 825 \circ C)$$

Storage:

- **Conditions**: Store in a tightly closed container in a cool, dry place.
- **Precautions**: Protect from moisture and incompatible substances such as acids.

Uses:

- **Medical**:
  - **Antacid**: Used to relieve symptoms of indigestion and heartburn by neutralizing stomach acid.
  - **Calcium Supplement**: Prescribed to prevent or treat calcium deficiencies and associated conditions such as osteoporosis.
- **Industrial**:
  - **Construction**: Used as a building material in the form of limestone and marble, and as a component of cement and concrete.

- **Paper and Plastic Industries**: Acts as a filler to improve the quality and reduce the cost of paper and plastic products.

- **Food Industry**: Used as a food additive (E170) to improve nutritional content and as a firming agent.

- **Agriculture**: Used to improve soil quality and adjust pH levels.

Official Preparation: Calcium Carbonate Tablets USP

- **Formulation**: Tablets typically contain 500 mg or 1,000 mg of calcium carbonate.

- **Usage**: Prescribed as an antacid or calcium supplement. Dosage varies based on the specific condition and patient needs.

- **Administration**: Tablets are taken orally, often with food to enhance absorption. For antacid use, tablets can be chewed or swallowed whole.

Storage of Official Preparations:

- **Tablets**: Store at room temperature in a tightly closed container, away from moisture and heat. Ensure the container is kept in a dry place to maintain tablet integrity.

ZINC EUGENOL CEMENT

Physical Properties:

- **Appearance**: A creamy, paste-like mixture when prepared, which sets to a hard mass.

- **Consistency**: Varies from a putty-like consistency when first mixed to a hard, durable material upon setting.

- **Color**: Typically pale yellow to white.

- **Odor**: Characteristic clove-like odor due to the presence of eugenol.

Preparation: Zinc eugenol cement is prepared by mixing zinc oxide powder with eugenol liquid. The preparation involves:

1. **Mixing**: The zinc oxide powder is mixed with eugenol on a glass slab or a mixing pad using a spatula.

2. **Proportions**: The typical ratio is about 3 parts zinc oxide to 1 part eugenol by weight, but this can vary depending on the desired consistency and application.

3. **Setting Time**: The mixture sets within a few minutes to several hours, depending on the exact formulation and environmental conditions like temperature and humidity.

Chemical Properties:

1. **Chemical Composition**: The primary components are zinc oxide (ZnO) and eugenol ($C_{10}H_{12}O_2$).

2. **Reactivity**: Eugenol, a phenolic compound, reacts with zinc oxide to form zinc eugenolate, a chelate compound that imparts the cement with its characteristic properties.

3. **Stability**: The set cement is stable under normal conditions but may degrade upon prolonged exposure to moisture or acidic environments.

Storage:

- **Conditions**: Store the zinc oxide powder and eugenol liquid separately in tightly sealed containers at room temperature.

- **Precautions**: Keep the materials in a cool, dry place away from direct sunlight and moisture. Properly seal containers to prevent contamination and degradation.

Uses:

- **Dental Applications**:
  - **Temporary Fillings**: Used as a temporary restorative material for teeth.
  - **Luting Agent**: Employed for temporary cementation of crowns, bridges, and other dental prosthetics.
  - **Base Material**: Acts as an insulating base under amalgam restorations to protect the pulp.

o **Endodontic Sealer**: Used in root canal therapy as a sealer due to its antimicrobial properties and soothing effect on the pulp.

- **Sedative Dressing**: Its soothing properties make it suitable for use as a sedative dressing in cases of pulpitis or sensitive teeth.

Official Preparation: Zinc Oxide-Eugenol Cement USP

1. **Formulation**: Typically available as a powder-liquid system, with zinc oxide powder in one container and eugenol liquid in another.

2. **Usage**: Proportions and mixing instructions are provided to achieve the desired consistency for specific dental applications.

3. **Administration**: Mixed on a glass slab or mixing pad using a spatula just before application.

Storage of Official Preparations:

1. **Zinc Oxide Powder**: Store in a tightly closed container at room temperature, away from moisture and heat.

2. **Eugenol Liquid**: Store in a tightly closed, light-resistant container at room temperature to prevent oxidation and degradation.

Zinc eugenol cement is commonly used in dentistry due to its soothing properties and versatility. It comes in several types, each tailored for specific applications. Here are the main types:

1. Type I Zinc Oxide-Eugenol Cement (Temporary Cement)

- **Composition**: Mainly zinc oxide and eugenol.

- **Uses**: Primarily used for temporary cementation of crowns, bridges, and inlays. Also used for temporary fillings.

- **Properties**: Sets quickly, providing sufficient strength for temporary applications. Easy to remove when necessary.

2. Type II Zinc Oxide-Eugenol Cement (Permanent Cement)

- **Composition**: Contains additives to improve strength and durability.

- **Uses**: Used for permanent cementation of crowns and bridges in certain cases where minimal biting forces are expected.

- **Properties**: Higher strength compared to Type I, but still less durable than other permanent cements.

3. Type III Zinc Oxide-Eugenol Cement (Base and Liner)

- **Composition**: Formulated to provide a thicker consistency for use as a base or liner under restorations.
- **Uses**: Applied as a base or liner under amalgam or composite restorations to provide thermal insulation and protect the pulp.
- **Properties**: Offers excellent thermal insulation and has a sedative effect on the pulp.

4. Type IV Zinc Oxide-Eugenol Cement (Intermediate Restorative Material)

- **Composition**: Contains higher proportions of zinc oxide and other fillers to enhance strength.
- **Uses**: Used as an intermediate restorative material for temporary restorations in situations where a longer-lasting temporary solution is required.
- **Properties**: Stronger and more durable than other types, suitable for temporary restorations that need to last for several months.

Reinforced Zinc Oxide-Eugenol Cement

- **Composition**: Contains resin or other reinforcing agents to enhance mechanical properties.
- **Uses**: Suitable for temporary and some permanent restorations where additional strength is needed.
- **Properties**: Improved compressive strength and durability compared to traditional zinc oxide-eugenol cements.

Eugenol-Free Zinc Oxide Cement

- **Composition**: Replaces eugenol with other oils like carboxylic acids to avoid eugenol's inhibitory effect on polymerization.

- **Uses**: Recommended for use under composite restorations or resin-based materials.
- **Properties**: Does not inhibit the setting of resin-based composites and adhesives, making it suitable for modern dental materials.

Each type of zinc eugenol cement is designed to address specific needs in dental practice, from temporary applications to providing a protective base for permanent restorations. Proper selection and application of the appropriate type ensure optimal outcomes in dental procedures.

CHAPTER – 9

ACIDIFER (ACIDIFYING AGENTS)

Mrs. Pooja Chauhan

Assistant Professor, Rajiv Gandhi Institute of Pharmacy, Faculty of Pharmaceutical Science & Technology, AKS University Satna, MP-India

ABSTRACT:

Acidifiers, or acidifying agents, are substances used to lower the pH of a solution, creating an acidic environment. These agents are crucial in various industries, including pharmaceuticals, food and beverage, and agriculture. In pharmaceuticals, acidifiers help to enhance the solubility and stability of certain drugs, ensuring their efficacy and shelf life. Common acidifying agents include citric acid, acetic acid, hydrochloric acid, and ascorbic acid. These acids are selected based on their compatibility with other components and the desired pH level of the final product. In the food and beverage industry, acidifiers not only enhance flavor but also act as preservatives by inhibiting microbial growth. They are used in products like soft drinks, sauces, and canned foods. In agriculture, acidifiers are added to animal feed to improve digestion and nutrient absorption by creating an optimal pH in the stomach. Acidifying agents also play a role in soil management, helping to adjust the pH of alkaline soils to make nutrients more accessible to plants. In industrial applications, acidifiers are used in cleaning agents and water treatment processes to remove scale and adjust pH levels. The effectiveness of acidifiers depends on their concentration, the buffering capacity of the solution, and the specific application requirements. Overall, acidifiers are versatile and essential for maintaining the desired pH levels across a wide range of applications, contributing to the functionality, stability, and safety of products.

GASTROINTESTINAL AGENTS

Gastrointestinal agents are the drugs which are used in treatment of gastrointestinal infection or disorders.

Inorganic compound are used to treat GI disorders:

1. To protective for intestinal inflammation.
2. It is used for altering the gastric pH.
3. It is used to adsorbents for intestinal toxins.
4. Laxative or cathartics for constipation.

AMMONIUM CHLORIDE

Molecular formula: NH_4Cl **Mol. Weight:** 53.49

Ammonium Chloride contains not less than 99.0 per cent and not more than 100.5 per cent of NH_4Cl, calculated on the dried basis

Physical Properties:

- **Appearance**: White crystalline solid or powder.
- **Molecular Weight**: 53.49 g/mol.
- **Melting Point**: Sublimes at 338 °C (640 °F).
- **Solubility**: Soluble in water (37.2 g/100 mL at 20 °C), slightly soluble in alcohol.
- **Density**: 1.527 g/cm^3.
- **Odor**: Odorless.
- **Taste**: Salty, cooling taste.
- **Crystal Structure**: Cubic crystal system.

Preparation:

Ammonium chloride can be prepared through several methods, including:

1. **By-Product of Soda Ash Production:**

Solvay Process: The primary industrial method involves the reaction of ammonia (NH_3) with hydrochloric acid (HCl) or as a by-product of the Solvay process for producing sodium carbonate (soda ash).

$$NH_3 + HCl \rightarrow NH_4Cl$$

2. **Direct Synthesis**:
   - **Neutralization Reaction**: Involves the direct neutralization of ammonia with hydrochloric acid.

$$NH_3 + HCl \rightarrow NH_4Cl$$

   - The reaction is exothermic and results in the formation of ammonium chloride as a solid product, which can be purified by recrystallization.

3. **Sublimation**:
   - **Sublimation of Solid Ammonium Chloride**: Heating solid ammonium chloride causes it to sublimate into ammonia and hydrogen chloride gases, which then recombine upon cooling to form pure ammonium chloride crystals.

Chemical Properties:

1. **Chemical Formula**: NH_4Cl.
2. **Acid-Base Properties**: Weakly acidic in solution due to hydrolysis.
3. **Decomposition**: Decomposes upon heating to release ammonia (NH_3) and hydrogen chloride (HCl) gases.

$$NH4Cl \rightarrow NH3 + HCl \ (\text{at } 338 \circ C)$$

4. **Reactivity**:
   - Reacts with strong bases to release ammonia gas:

$$NH_4Cl + NaOH \rightarrow NH_3 + H_2O + NaCl$$

- o Reacts with nitrates and other oxidizing agents under certain conditions.

Storage:

1. **Conditions**: Store in a cool, dry place in tightly closed containers to prevent moisture absorption.
2. **Precautions**: Protect from incompatible substances like strong acids and bases. Store away from sources of heat and ignition.
3. **Handling**: Use personal protective equipment (PPE) such as gloves and safety goggles when handling. Ensure good ventilation in storage and handling areas to avoid dust accumulation.

Uses:

1. **Pharmaceutical**:
   - **Expectorant**: Used in cough syrups and other formulations to thin and loosen mucus in the respiratory tract.
   - **Systemic Acidifier**: Helps to acidify urine in the treatment of certain medical conditions.
2. **Food Industry**:
   - **Leavening Agent**: Used in baking to aid in the rising of baked goods.
   - **Nutrient Supplement**: Provides a source of nitrogen in nutritional supplements and food products.
3. **Industrial Applications**:
   - **Metalwork**: Employed in the electroplating and metal refining industries.
   - **Textiles and Dyeing**: Used as a mordant in dyeing processes and as a flux in textile printing.

- **Batteries**: Used in dry cell batteries as an electrolyte component.

4. **Agriculture**:
   - **Fertilizer**: Provides nitrogen for plant growth and soil conditioning.

5. **Laboratory**:
   - **Buffer Solutions**: Used in buffer solutions to maintain a stable pH in chemical reactions and biological research.

Official Preparation:

Ammonium Chloride Oral Solution USP

1. **Formulation**: Contains ammonium chloride in a solution form, typically at a concentration of 100 mg/mL.
2. **Usage**: Administered orally as an expectorant or systemic acidifier.
3. **Dosage**: Dosage varies depending on the specific medical condition and patient needs. Commonly prescribed doses range from 1-4 grams per day in divided doses.
4. **Administration**: Typically taken with or after meals to minimize gastrointestinal discomfort. The solution can be mixed with water or juice to improve palatability.
5. **Packaging**: Supplied in bottles with clear labeling, including concentration, dosage instructions, and storage requirements.

Storage of Official Preparations:

- **Conditions**: Store at room temperature, typically between 15-30 °C (59-86 °F). Protect from light and moisture.
- **Precautions**: Keep out of reach of children. Follow the expiration date and discard any unused solution after the expiration date.

Patient Information:

1. **Side Effects**: Possible side effects include nausea, vomiting, and stomach upset. Inform healthcare providers of any persistent or severe side effects.
2. **Contraindications**: Patients with renal impairment, metabolic or respiratory acidosis should use ammonium chloride with caution and under medical supervision.
3. **Interactions**: Inform healthcare providers of all medications and supplements being taken to avoid potential interactions.

HYDROCHLORIC ACID

Chemical formula: HCl   **Mol. Weight:** 36.46

Hydrochloric acid is a solution of hydrogen chloride gas (HCl) in water.

Dilute Hydrochloric Acid is prepared by mixing 274 g of Hydrochloric Acid and 726 g of Purified Water.

Dilute Hydrochloric Acid contains not less than 9.5 per cent and not more than 10.5 per cent w/w of HCl.

Synonyms: Muriatic acid

Physical Properties:

- **Appearance**: Colorless to slightly yellow liquid with a pungent odor.
- **Molecular Weight**: 36.46 g/mol.
- **Boiling Point**: Approximately 110 °C (230 °F) for a 20% solution.
- **Melting Point**: -27.32 °C (-17.18 °F) for a 37% solution.
- **Density**: 1.18 g/cm³ for a 37% solution.
- **Solubility**: Miscible with water, forming a strong acidic solution. Also soluble in alcohol and ether.
- **pH**: Highly acidic, with a pH less than 1 for concentrated solutions.

Preparation: Hydrochloric acid can be prepared through several methods, including:

1. **Synthesis from Hydrogen and Chlorine**:

- o Direct combination of hydrogen gas (H_2) and chlorine gas (Cl_2) in the presence of UV light to form hydrogen chloride gas, which is then dissolved in water to form hydrochloric acid.

$$H_2 + Cl_2 \rightarrow 2HCl$$

2. **By-Product of Chlor-Alkali Process**:
   - o In the industrial chlor-alkali process, electrolysis of sodium chloride ($NaCl$) solution produces chlorine gas, which can be combined with hydrogen gas to produce hydrochloric acid.

3. **Reaction of Sulfuric Acid with Sodium Chloride**:
   - o Historically, hydrochloric acid was produced by reacting sulfuric acid (H_2SO_4) with sodium chloride ($NaCl$).

$$NaCl + H_2SO_4 \rightarrow HCl + NaHSO_4$$

Chemical Properties:

- **Chemical Formula**: HCl (in aqueous solution).
- **Acid Strength**: Strong acid, dissociates completely in water to release hydrogen ions (H^+) and chloride ions (Cl^-).
- **Reactivity**:
  - o Reacts with bases to form salts and water:

$$HCl + NaOH \rightarrow NaCl + H_2O$$

  - o Reacts with metals to produce hydrogen gas and metal chlorides:

$$Zn + 2HCl \rightarrow ZnCl_2 + H_2$$

  - o Reacts with carbonates and bicarbonates to release carbon dioxide gas:

$$CaCO_3 + 2HCl \rightarrow CaCl_2 + H_2O + CO_2$$

Storage:

- **Conditions**: Store in a tightly closed container made of corrosion-resistant materials, such as glass or certain plastics. Keep in a cool, well-ventilated area away from incompatible substances.

- **Precautions**: Avoid exposure to heat, moisture, and direct sunlight. Use appropriate personal protective equipment (PPE), including gloves, goggles, and acid-resistant clothing, when handling.

Uses:

1. **Industrial Applications**:
   - **Metal Processing**: Used for pickling of steel to remove rust and scale.
   - **Production of Inorganic Compounds**: Involved in the production of various chlorides, such as polyvinyl chloride (PVC) and calcium chloride.
   - **pH Regulation**: Used to adjust the pH of process water streams.
   - **Food Industry**: Employed in the production of gelatin and as an acidulant in food processing.

2. **Laboratory Applications**:
   - **Reagent**: Used as a reagent in chemical analysis and titrations.
   - **Cleaning Agent**: Utilized for cleaning glassware and equipment due to its ability to dissolve mineral deposits and organic matter.

3. **Medical Applications**:
   - **Digestive Aid**: Hydrochloric acid is naturally present in the stomach and is essential for digestion and absorption of nutrients. It is sometimes used in preparations to treat conditions related to low stomach acidity.

Official Preparation: Hydrochloric Acid Solution USP

- **Formulation**: Typically available in concentrations ranging from 10% to 37% by weight.
- **Usage**: Used as a reagent and for pH adjustment in pharmaceutical formulations.
- **Dosage**: Concentration and volume depend on the specific application and desired pH adjustment.

- **Administration**: Used in laboratory and industrial processes, not for direct medicinal ingestion.

Storage of Official Preparations:

- **Conditions**: Store in a cool, dry place in tightly closed containers. Use containers made of materials resistant to corrosion, such as glass or specific plastics.
- **Precautions**: Label containers clearly with concentration and hazard information. Ensure proper ventilation in storage areas to prevent accumulation of fumes.

Safety Information:

- **Hazards**: Highly corrosive, can cause severe burns to skin and eyes. Inhalation of vapors can irritate respiratory tract.
- **First Aid**:
    - **Skin Contact**: Rinse immediately with plenty of water for at least 15 minutes. Seek medical attention if irritation persists.
    - **Eye Contact**: Rinse immediately with plenty of water for at least 15 minutes. Seek medical attention immediately.
    - **Inhalation**: Move to fresh air. If breathing is difficult, provide oxygen and seek medical attention.
    - **Ingestion**: Do not induce vomiting. Rinse mouth with water and seek medical attention immediately.

CHAPTER – 10

ANATACID

Mr. Satyendra Garg

Assistant Professor, Rajiv Gandhi Institute of Pharmacy, Faculty of

Pharmaceutical Science & Technology, AKS University Satna, MP-India

ABSTRACT:

Antacids are medications used to neutralize stomach acid and provide relief from heartburn, indigestion, and other symptoms associated with excess gastric acid. They work by raising the pH level in the stomach, reducing acidity and alleviating discomfort. Common active ingredients in antacids include calcium carbonate, magnesium hydroxide, aluminum hydroxide, and sodium bicarbonate. These compounds react with hydrochloric acid in the stomach to form water and other neutral compounds, providing quick symptom relief. Antacids are available in various forms, such as tablets, chewable tablets, powders, and liquids, making them convenient for different preferences and situations. In addition to their use in treating occasional heartburn, antacids are often recommended for conditions like gastroesophageal reflux disease (GERD) and peptic ulcers. However, they are intended for short-term relief and not as a substitute for long-term management of chronic acid-related disorders. Overuse of antacids can lead to side effects such as constipation or diarrhea, depending on the active ingredients. It's also important to be aware of potential interactions with other medications, as antacids can affect the absorption of certain drugs. Consulting a healthcare professional before starting any antacid regimen is advisable, especially for individuals with underlying health conditions or those taking other medications.

Introduction:

Antacids are substances which on ingestion react with the gastric acid and reduce the acidity of gastric contents.

ANTACID

1. Neutralize excess HCl which causes pain andpossible ulceration.
2. Inactivate the proteolytic enzyme or pepsin.
3. Stomach pH range from 1 when empty and 7 if food is present.
4. Low acid pH is due to the presence of endogenous HCl.
5. Alkaline bases used to neutralize excess HClassociated with gastritis and peptic ulcers
6. No antacid is "ideal", but there are criterion that have been developed
   - It should not be adsorbable or causesystemic alkalosis
   - It should not be a laxative or causeconstipation
   - It should exert the effect rapidly andover a long period of time
   - The reaction with gastric HCl shouldnot cause a large evolution of gas
   - It should buffer in the pH of 4-6 range
   - It should probably inhibit pepsin.

Classification of antacid:

1. Systemic antacid (absorbable antacid): Sodium bicrbonate
2. Non-systematic antacid (Non-absorable antacid):
   - Aluminum hydroxide,
   - Magnesium carbonate, magnesium oxide, magnesium hydroxide and magnesium trisilicate.
   - Combination antacid preparation: aluminium hydroxide gel and magnesium hydroxide; aluminium hydroxide gel and magnesium trisilicate, megaldrate,

Mechanism of action: Neutralizes excess stomach acids

Side effects:

- Constipation and hypophosphatemia (aluminum hydroxide);

- Diarrhea and hypermagnesemia (magnesium hydroxide).

Antacid produces:

- Relieve in heart burn
- Relieve pain
- Reduce spasm
- Relieve from the uncomfortable feeling from overeating and a growing hungry feeling between meals.

Classification of antacid:

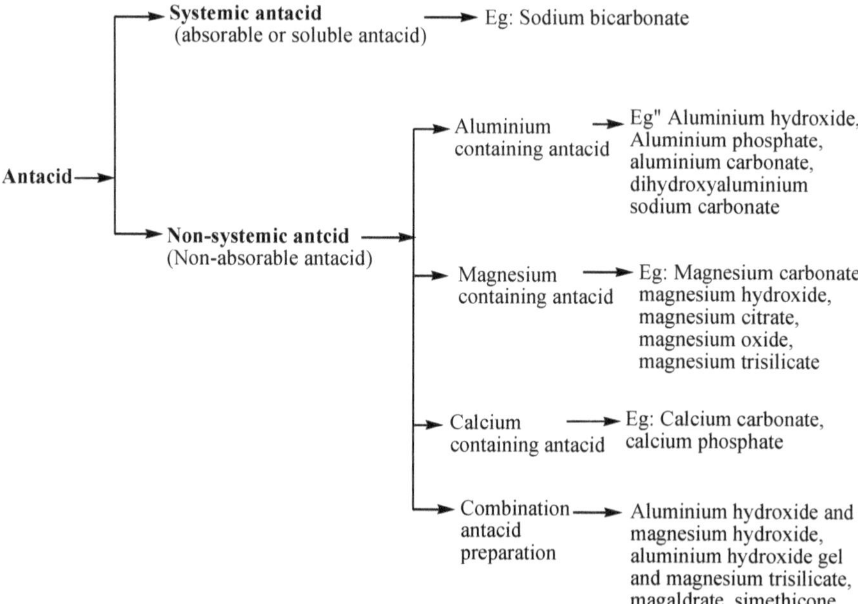

Idea properties of antacid:

1. It should be quick in action.
2. It should not produce systemic alkalosis.
3. It should not interfere in absorption of food.
4. It should be pleasant and cheap.

5. It should have good patient acceptability.

SODIUM BICARBONATE

Chemical formula: $NaHCO_3$ **Mol. Weight**: 84

Synonyms: Baking soda, Metha soda

Physical Properties:

- **Appearance**: White crystalline powder or granules.
- **Molecular Weight**: 84.01 g/mol.
- **Melting Point**: Decomposes at about 50 °C to 100 °C.
- **Solubility**: Soluble in water (9.6 g/100 mL at 20 °C), insoluble in alcohol.
- **Density**: 2.20 g/cm³.
- **Taste**: Slightly alkaline and salty taste.

Preparation: Sodium bicarbonate can be prepared by several methods:

1. **Solvay Process**:
   - The most common industrial method involves the reaction of sodium chloride ($NaCl$), ammonia (NH_3), and carbon dioxide (CO_2) in water.

$$NaCl + NH_3 + CO_2 + H_2O \rightarrow NaHCO3 + NH_4Cl$$

   - The sodium bicarbonate precipitates out and is filtered and dried.

2. **Reaction of Sodium Carbonate with Carbon Dioxide**:
   - Another method is the reaction of sodium carbonate (Na_2CO_3) with carbon dioxide and water.

$$Na_2CO_3 + CO2 + H_2O \rightarrow 2NaHCO_3$$

Chemical Properties:

- **Chemical Formula**: $NaHCO_3$.
- **Reactivity**:
   - **Acid-Base Reactions**: Acts as a weak base and reacts with acids to form carbon dioxide, water, and a salt.

$$NaHCO_3 + HCl \rightarrow NaCl + H_2O + CO_2$$

- o **Thermal Decomposition**: Decomposes upon heating to form sodium carbonate, water, and carbon dioxide.

$$2NaHCO_3 \rightarrow Na_2CO_3 + H_2O + CO_2$$

- **Buffering**: Acts as a buffer to maintain pH in solutions by neutralizing acids and bases.

Storage:

- **Conditions**: Store in a tightly closed container in a cool, dry place.
- **Precautions**: Protect from moisture and acidic vapors. Store away from strong acids and bases.

Uses:

1. **Medical**:
   - o **Antacid**: Used to relieve heartburn, indigestion, and upset stomach by neutralizing stomach acid.
   - o **Alkalinizing Agent**: Used to treat metabolic acidosis and certain drug overdoses.
   - o **Topical Applications**: Used in pastes for treating insect bites, stings, and minor burns.

2. **Food Industry**:
   - o **Leavening Agent**: Used in baking to release carbon dioxide and cause dough to rise.
   - o **Food Additive**: Used to regulate acidity in food products.

3. **Cleaning Agent**:
   - o **Mild Abrasive**: Used in household cleaning products for its mild abrasive properties.
   - o **Deodorizer**: Used to neutralize odors in refrigerators and other enclosed spaces.

4. **Industrial Applications**:

-   ○ **pH Control**: Used in water treatment and various chemical processes to control pH levels.

Official Preparation: Sodium Bicarbonate Tablets USP

- **Formulation**: Tablets typically contain 325 mg to 650 mg of sodium bicarbonate.
- **Usage**: Prescribed for relief of acid indigestion, heartburn, and to alkalize urine in specific medical conditions.
- **Dosage**: Varies based on the condition being treated. For antacid use, typically 1-2 tablets every 4 hours as needed, not exceeding the recommended daily limit.
- **Administration**: Tablets should be taken with a full glass of water.

Storage of Official Preparations:

- **Conditions**: Store at room temperature, away from moisture and heat. Ensure the container is tightly closed to protect from humidity.
- **Precautions**: Follow expiration dates and storage instructions as provided by the manufacturer. Keep out of reach of children.

Safety Information:

- **Side Effects**: May include stomach cramps, increased thirst, and gas. Overuse can lead to alkalosis and electrolyte imbalance.
- **Contraindications**: Patients with hypertension, kidney disease, or a history of electrolyte imbalances should use sodium bicarbonate with caution and under medical supervision.
- **Interactions**: Inform healthcare providers of all medications being taken, as sodium bicarbonate can interact with certain drugs, affecting their absorption or efficacy.

ALUMINIUM HYDROXIDE GEL

Mol. Formula: $Al(OH)_3$ **Mol. Weight:** 77.99

It is available in the two forms:

1. Aluminium hydroxide gel:

   - Aqueous white viscous suspension of hydrated aluminium oxide with varying amount of aluminium carbonate (>3.5%) and aluminium oxide (<4.4%).
   - Contain sodium benzoate as preservative, oil of menthe, glycerin or sucrose as sweetening agents.
   - Small amount of water/ clear liquid may separate on standing.
   - pH is between 5.5 and 8.0.

2. Dried aluminium hydroxide gel:

   - It is a white, odourless, tasteless amorphous powder.
   - It is insoluble in water and alcohol.
   - It is soluble in dilute mineral acid and solution of fixed alkali hydroxide.

Physical Properties:

- **Appearance**: White, viscous, gelatinous suspension.
- **Molecular Weight**: 78.00 g/mol.
- **Solubility**: Insoluble in water and alcohol; soluble in mineral acids and sodium hydroxide.
- **Density**: Approximately 2.42 g/cm^3.
- **Odor and Taste**: Odorless, tasteless.

Preparation: Aluminium hydroxide gel can be prepared by:

1. **Precipitation Method**:

   - Mixing a solution of aluminium salt, such as aluminium chloride ($AlCl_3$) or aluminium sulfate ($Al_2(SO_4)_3$), with a base like ammonium hydroxide (NH_4OH).

$$AlCl_3 + 3NH_4OH \rightarrow Al(OH)_3 + 3NH_4Cl$$

   - The precipitated aluminium hydroxide is washed and collected to form the gel.

Chemical Properties:

- **Chemical Formula**: $Al(OH)_3$.
- **Reactivity**:
  - **Amphoteric Nature**: Reacts with both acids and bases. $Al(OH)_3 + 3HCl \rightarrow AlCl_3 + 3H_2O$
  - **Decomposition**: Decomposes upon heating to form aluminium oxide and water.

Storage:

- **Conditions**: Store in a tightly closed container at room temperature.
- **Precautions**: Protect from freezing and excessive heat.

Uses:

1. **Medical**:
   - **Antacid**: Neutralizes stomach acid and relieves symptoms of indigestion, heartburn, and peptic ulcers.
   - **Phosphate Binder**: Used to reduce phosphate levels in patients with kidney disease.
2. **Industrial**:
   - **Water Purification**: Used as a coagulant in water treatment processes.
   - **Cosmetics**: Utilized in various cosmetic formulations for its soothing properties.

Official Preparation: Aluminium Hydroxide Gel USP

1. **Formulation**: Available as a suspension containing aluminium hydroxide equivalent to 320 mg of aluminium oxide per 5 mL.
2. **Usage**: Used as an antacid to neutralize stomach acid.
3. **Dosage**: Typically, 5-10 mL taken between meals and at bedtime.
4. **Administration**: Taken orally, often mixed with water or other liquids.

Storage of Official Preparations:

- **Conditions**: Store at room temperature in a tightly closed container.

- **Precautions**: Shake well before use to ensure proper suspension. Keep out of reach of children.

MAGNESIUM OXIDE

Mol. Formula: MgO   **Mol. Weight**: 40.3

Synonyms: Magnesia

It contains not less than 98.0% of MgO.

Physical Properties:

- **Appearance**: White powder or crystalline solid.
- **Molecular Weight**: 40.30 g/mol.
- **Melting Point**: 2,852 °C (5,166 °F).
- **Boiling Point**: 3,600 °C (6,512 °F).
- **Solubility**: Slightly soluble in water; more soluble in acids.
- **Density**: 3.58 g/cm³.
- **Odor and Taste**: Odorless, slightly alkaline taste.

Preparation: Magnesium oxide can be prepared by:

1. **Calcination of Magnesium Carbonate**:
   - Heating magnesium carbonate ($MgCO_3$) decomposes it into magnesium oxide and carbon dioxide.
     $MgCO_3 \rightarrow MgO + CO_2$ (at 350–800°C)

2. **Thermal Decomposition of Magnesium Hydroxide**:
   - Heating magnesium hydroxide ($Mg(OH)_2$) produces magnesium oxide and water. $Mg(OH)2 \rightarrow MgO + H2O$ (at 350–500°C)

Chemical Properties:

- **Chemical Formula**: MgO.
- **Reactivity**:

- o **Basic Nature**: Reacts with acids to form magnesium salts and water. $MgO+2HCl{\rightarrow}MgCl_2+H_2O$
  - o **Hydration**: Reacts with water to form magnesium hydroxide. $MgO+H_2O{\rightarrow}Mg(OH)_2$

Storage:

- **Conditions**: Store in a tightly closed container in a cool, dry place.
- **Precautions**: Protect from moisture as it can react with water to form magnesium hydroxide.

Uses:

1. **Medical**:
   - o **Antacid**: Neutralizes stomach acid and relieves indigestion and heartburn.
   - o **Laxative**: Used to relieve constipation by drawing water into the intestines.

2. **Industrial**:
   - o **Refractory Material**: Used in furnace linings and crucibles due to its high melting point.
   - o **Agriculture**: Used to correct soil acidity and provide magnesium for plant nutrition.

3. **Food Industry**:
   - o **Food Additive**: Used as an anti-caking agent and dietary supplement.

Official Preparation: Magnesium Oxide Tablets USP

- **Formulation**: Tablets containing 200 mg to 400 mg of magnesium oxide.
- **Usage**: Used as an antacid and magnesium supplement.
- **Dosage**: Typically 250 mg to 500 mg daily, or as directed by a healthcare provider.
- **Administration**: Taken orally with a full glass of water.

Storage of Official Preparations:

- **Conditions**: Store at room temperature in a tightly closed container.
- **Precautions**: Keep out of reach of children and avoid exposure to moisture.

MAGNESIUM TRISILICATE

Mol. Formula: $(2MgO.3SiO_2.xH_2O)$ or $(MgSiO_3)_2SiO_2.xH_2O$

Mol. Weight: Anhydrous 260.86

Physical Properties:
- **Appearance**: White, fine, odorless powder.
- **Molecular Weight**: Approximately 260.86 g/mol.
- **Solubility**: Practically insoluble in water and alcohol; soluble in dilute acids.
- **Density**: Around 2.96 g/cm³.
- **Taste**: Tasteless.

Preparation: Magnesium trisilicate is prepared by the reaction of magnesium salts, such as magnesium sulfate ($MgSO_4$) or magnesium chloride ($MgCl_2$), with sodium silicate (Na_2SiO_3):

$$3MgCl_2 + Na_2SiO3 + 3H_2O \rightarrow Mg_2Si_3O_8 + 2NaCl$$

The resulting precipitate of magnesium trisilicate is then filtered, washed, and dried to obtain the final product.

Chemical Properties:
- **Chemical Formula**: $Mg_2Si_3O_8 \cdot xH_2O$ (often hydrated).
- **Reactivity**: Reacts with acids to form soluble magnesium salts and colloidal silica.
- **Stability**: Chemically stable under normal conditions; does not decompose readily at room temperature.

Storage:
- **Conditions**: Store in a tightly closed container in a cool, dry place.

- **Precautions**: Protect from moisture and contamination. Keep away from strong acids and bases.

Uses:

1. **Medical**:
   - o **Antacid**: Neutralizes stomach acid, providing relief from indigestion, heartburn, and peptic ulcers. It acts more slowly than some other antacids but has a prolonged effect.
   - o **Protective Agent**: Forms a protective coating on the stomach lining, helping to prevent and heal ulcers.
2. **Food Industry**:
   - o **Food Additive**: Occasionally used as an anti-caking agent in powdered food products.
3. **Cosmetics**:
   - o **Abrasive and Bulking Agent**: Used in certain cosmetic formulations for its texture and absorptive properties.

Official Preparation: Magnesium Trisilicate Mixture BP

- **Formulation**: Typically available as a suspension, containing magnesium trisilicate along with other excipients to enhance its stability and palatability.
- **Usage**: Used as an antacid to relieve symptoms of dyspepsia, gastritis, and peptic ulcers.
- **Dosage**: The standard dose is 5-10 mL taken one to three hours after meals and at bedtime, or as directed by a healthcare provider.
- **Administration**: Shake well before use to ensure uniform suspension. The mixture can be taken with or without water.

Storage of Official Preparations:

- **Conditions**: Store at room temperature in a tightly closed container.
- **Precautions**: Protect from light and moisture. Ensure the container is kept upright and securely closed to prevent spillage and contamination.

Follow expiration dates and discard any unused portion after the expiration date.

Safety Information:

- **Side Effects**: Generally well-tolerated, but may cause constipation or diarrhea in some individuals. Prolonged use may lead to imbalances in electrolytes, particularly magnesium and phosphate levels.

- **Contraindications**: Not recommended for individuals with severe kidney disease or hypersensitivity to magnesium trisilicate. Use with caution in patients with electrolyte imbalances or dehydration.

- **Interactions**: Can affect the absorption of other medications, so it is advisable to take other drugs either 1-2 hours before or after taking magnesium trisilicate.

CHAPTER – 11

CATHERTICS

Mrs. Neelam Singh

Assistant Professor, Rajiv Gandhi Institute of Pharmacy, Faculty of
Pharmaceutical Science & Technology, AKS University Satna, MP-India

ABSTRACT:

Cathartics, also known as laxatives, are substances used to stimulate
bowel movements and relieve constipation. They work by different
mechanisms, including increasing intestinal motility, softening stool, and
drawing water into the intestines to facilitate the passage of feces. Common
types of cathartics include bulk-forming agents, osmotic laxatives, stimulant
laxatives, and stool softeners. Bulk-forming agents like psyllium absorb water
and swell, adding bulk to the stool and promoting peristalsis. Osmotic laxatives,
such as polyethylene glycol and lactulose, attract water into the colon, softening
stools and increasing bowel movements. Stimulant laxatives, including senna
and bisacodyl, directly stimulate the intestinal muscles to contract, accelerating
stool transit. Stool softeners, like docusate sodium, help mix water into the
stool, making it easier to pass. Cathartics are often used to prepare patients for
diagnostic procedures such as colonoscopies, or to manage chronic constipation
in certain medical conditions. While generally effective, overuse or misuse of
cathartics can lead to dehydration, electrolyte imbalances, and dependence.
Therefore, they should be used under medical supervision, and patients should
be encouraged to adopt healthy dietary and lifestyle practices to maintain
regular bowel movements.

Introduction:

Saline cathartics or purgatives are agents that quicken and increase
evacuation from the bowl.

Cathartics are used:

1. To ease defecation in patients with painful hemorrhoids or other rectal disorders and to avoid excessive straining and concurrent increase in abdominal pressure in patients with hernias Or
2. To avoid potentially hazardous rise in B.P. during defecation in patients with hypertension, cerebral coronary or other arterial disease Or
3. To relieve acute constipation Or
4. To remove solid material from intestinal tract prior to certain roentgenographic studies.

Laxative should only be used for short term therapy as prolonged use may lead to loss of spontaneous bowl rhythm upon which normal evacuation depends, causing patient to become dependent on laxatives, the so called laxative effect.

Constipation is the infrequent or difficult evacuation of the feces. It may be due to a person resisting the natural urge to defecate, causing the fecal material which remains in the colon to lose fluid and to become relatively dry and hard. Constipation can also be due to intestinal atony, intestinal spasm, emotions, drugs and diet.

Types of laxatives

1. Stimulants
2. Bulk forming
3. Emollient
4. Saline cathartics

1. Stimulants act by local irritation on the intestinal tract which increase peristaltic activity. They include phenolphthalein, aloin, cascara extract, rhubarb extract, senna extract, podophyllin, castor oil, bisacodyl, calomel etc.
2. Bulk forming laxatives are made from cellulose, sodium carboxyl methyl cellulose and karaya gum.

3. The emollient laxatives act either as lubricants facilitating the passage of compacted fecal material or as stool softeners. E.g mineral oil, d-octyl sodium sulfosuccinate, an anionic surface active agent.

4. Saline cathartics act by increasing the osmotic load of the GIT.

DISODIUM HYDROGEN PHOSPHATE

Synonyms: Sodium orthophosphate

Mol. Formula: $Na_2HPO_4.12H_2O$ **Mol.Wt.:** 354.14

Physical Properties:

- **Appearance**: White, odorless crystalline powder or granules.
- **Molecular Weight**: 141.96 g/mol (anhydrous form), 268.07 g/mol (heptahydrate).
- **Solubility**: Highly soluble in water (7.7 g/100 mL at 20 °C for the anhydrous form); insoluble in alcohol.
- **Density**: 1.67 g/cm³ (anhydrous).
- **Melting Point**: Decomposes at high temperatures without a distinct melting point.

Preparation: Disodium hydrogen phosphate can be prepared by neutralizing phosphoric acid (H_3PO_4) with sodium hydroxide (NaOH):

$$H_3PO_4 + 2NaOH \rightarrow Na_2HPO_4 + 2H_2O$$

The resulting solution is then evaporated to crystallize the disodium hydrogen phosphate.

Chemical Properties:

- **Chemical Formula**: Na_2HPO_4.
- **Reactivity**: Acts as a mild alkali. Reacts with acids to form sodium dihydrogen phosphate (NaH_2PO_4) and with bases to form trisodium phosphate (Na_3PO_4).
- **Stability**: Stable under normal conditions but should be protected from moisture to prevent caking and degradation.

Storage:

- **Conditions**: Store in a tightly closed container in a cool, dry place.
- **Precautions**: Protect from moisture and strong acids or bases.

Uses:

1. **Medical**: Used as a saline laxative and in some buffered saline solutions for kidney dialysis.
2. **Food Industry**: Used as an emulsifier, thickening agent, and pH buffer in processed foods.
3. **Water Treatment**: Used to prevent pipe corrosion and scaling.
4. **Laboratory**: Used in buffer solutions to maintain pH.

Official Preparation: Disodium Hydrogen Phosphate Tablets USP

- **Formulation**: Typically available in various hydrated forms.
- **Usage**: Used as a saline laxative or as a component in oral rehydration salts.
- **Dosage**: Dosage varies depending on the specific use and patient requirements.
- **Administration**: Taken orally, dissolved in water.

Storage of Official Preparations:

- **Conditions**: Store at room temperature in a tightly closed container.
- **Precautions**: Keep away from moisture and heat. Follow expiration dates and usage instructions.

MAGNISEUM SULPHATE

Mol. Formula: $MgSO_4$ **Mol. Wt.:** 246.50

Physical Properties:

- **Appearance**: Colorless, odorless crystalline solid or white powder.
- **Molecular Weight**: 120.37 g/mol (anhydrous), 246.48 g/mol (heptahydrate).
- **Solubility**: Highly soluble in water (710 g/L at 20 °C for the heptahydrate); slightly soluble in alcohol.

- **Density**: 2.66 g/cm³ (anhydrous), 1.68 g/cm³ (heptahydrate).
- **Melting Point**: 1124 °C (2055 °F) for the anhydrous form; heptahydrate decomposes at around 150 °C.

Preparation: Magnesium sulphate can be prepared by neutralizing magnesium oxide (MgO) or magnesium carbonate ($MgCO_3$) with sulfuric acid (H_2SO_4):

$$MgO + H_2SO_4 \rightarrow MgSO_4 + H_2O$$

or

$$MgCO_3 + {}_{H2SO4} \rightarrow MgSO_4 + CO_2 + H_2O$$

The resulting solution is then evaporated to obtain the desired crystalline form.

Chemical Properties:

- **Chemical Formula**: $MgSO_4$.
- **Reactivity**: Reacts with alkali metal hydroxides to form insoluble magnesium hydroxide.
- **Stability**: Stable under normal conditions. The hydrated forms can lose water upon heating.

Storage:

- **Conditions**: Store in a tightly closed container in a cool, dry place.
- **Precautions**: Protect from moisture to prevent caking and degradation.

Uses:

1. **Medical**:
   - **Laxative**: Used to relieve occasional constipation.
   - **Epsom Salt**: Used for soaking baths to relieve sore muscles and as a skin softener.
   - **Magnesium Supplement**: Used to treat magnesium deficiency.
2. **Agriculture**: Used as a magnesium fertilizer to correct soil magnesium deficiency.
3. **Industrial**: Used in the production of textiles and in the tanning and dyeing of leather.
4. **Laboratory**: Used in various chemical reactions and as a drying agent.

Official Preparation: Magnesium Sulphate Injection USP

- **Formulation**: Available as a sterile solution for intravenous or intramuscular injection.
- **Usage**: Used to treat eclampsia, pre-eclampsia, and magnesium deficiency.
- **Dosage**: Dosage varies depending on the specific medical condition being treated.
- **Administration**: Administered by healthcare professionals in a clinical setting.

Storage of Official Preparations:

- **Conditions**: Store at room temperature in a tightly closed container.
- **Precautions**: Protect from light and moisture. Follow expiration dates and usage instructions.

KAOLIN

Synonyms: Bolus Alba; China clay; White bole; Argilla, Porcelain clay; Hin-Chiknimati.

They are derived from pegmetities or from hydrothermal alterations along fractures. They may also occur as blanket deposits in extensive areas of igneous of metamorphic rocks, bedded deposits derived from feelspathic, sandstones or as pockets in limestones.

Physical Properties:

- **Appearance**: White to yellowish or grayish fine powder.
- **Molecular Weight**: Approximately 258.16 g/mol.
- **Solubility**: Insoluble in water and organic solvents; slightly soluble in acids.
- **Density**: About 2.6 g/cm³.
- **Odor and Taste**: Odorless and tasteless.
- **Crystal Structure**: Typically platy or flaky.

Preparation: Kaolin is a naturally occurring clay mineral primarily composed of the mineral kaolinite ($Al_2Si_2O_5(OH)_4$). It is prepared by:

1. **Mining**: Extracted from open-pit mines.
2. **Processing**:
   - **Crushing and Grinding**: The raw kaolin is crushed and ground to a fine powder.
   - **Beneficiation**: Impurities are removed through techniques such as flotation, magnetic separation, and chemical treatment.
   - **Drying**: The processed kaolin is dried to remove moisture.
   - **Pulverization**: Further ground to achieve the desired particle size and consistency.

Chemical Properties:

- **Chemical Formula**: $Al_2Si_2O_5(OH)_4$.
- **Reactivity**: Chemically inert under normal conditions. Can react with strong acids and bases.
- **Stability**: Stable under normal conditions; resistant to heat and chemical attack.

Storage:

- **Conditions**: Store in a cool, dry place in tightly closed containers to prevent contamination.
- **Precautions**: Protect from moisture and dust. Use appropriate personal protective equipment (PPE) to avoid inhalation of dust.

Uses:

1. **Medical**:
   - **Antidiarrheal**: Used in the treatment of diarrhea by adsorbing toxins and increasing the bulk of stool.
   - **Topical Applications**: Used in creams and ointments to treat skin irritations and protect the skin.
2. **Cosmetics**:

o **Face Masks and Powders**: Used for its absorbent and soothing properties.

3. **Industrial**:

   o **Paper Coating**: Used as a coating and filler to improve the appearance and printability of paper.

   o **Ceramics**: Utilized in the production of porcelain and other ceramics.

   o **Paints and Coatings**: Acts as an extender and provides desirable rheological properties.

4. **Agriculture**: Used as a carrier for pesticides and fertilizers.

Official Preparation: Kaolin and Pectin Suspension USP

- **Formulation**: A suspension containing kaolin and pectin, used as an antidiarrheal agent.

- **Usage**: Prescribed to treat diarrhea and gastrointestinal discomfort by adsorbing toxins and soothing the gut lining.

- **Dosage**: Typically, 30-120 mL taken orally after each loose bowel movement. Dosage may vary based on patient needs and medical advice.

- **Administration**: Shake well before use. The suspension is taken orally, usually with water or as directed by a healthcare provider.

Storage of Official Preparations:

- **Conditions**: Store at room temperature in a tightly closed container.

- **Precautions**: Protect from light and moisture. Ensure the container is kept upright and securely closed to prevent spillage and contamination. Follow expiration dates and usage instructions.

Safety Information:

- **Side Effects**: Generally well-tolerated. Possible side effects include constipation and, rarely, allergic reactions.

- **Contraindications**: Not recommended for individuals with known hypersensitivity to kaolin or any components of the formulation.

- **Interactions**: Inform healthcare providers of all medications being taken, as kaolin can adsorb and reduce the effectiveness of certain drugs.

BENTONITE

Source: Bentonite is mineral deposited closely resembling clay; it was formed by the weathering of volcanic ash.

Physical Properties:

- **Appearance**: Cream to grayish powder or granules.
- **Molecular Weight**: Variable, approximately 360 g/mol (depends on the specific composition).
- **Solubility**: Insoluble in water but swells and forms a gel-like substance; insoluble in organic solvents.
- **Density**: Approximately 2.6 - 2.7 g/cm^3.
- **Odor and Taste**: Odorless and tasteless.
- **Crystal Structure**: Plate-like, layered structure.

Preparation: Bentonite is a naturally occurring clay derived from the weathering of volcanic ash. It is primarily composed of montmorillonite and is prepared through:

1. **Mining**: Extracted from bentonite deposits.
2. **Processing**:
   - **Drying**: The raw bentonite is dried to reduce moisture content.
   - **Grinding**: The dried bentonite is ground to a fine powder.
   - **Purification**: Impurities are removed through techniques such as sieving, sedimentation, and sometimes chemical treatment to improve its quality and performance.

Chemical Properties:

Chemical Formula: Predominantly

$(Na,Ca)_{0.3}(Al,Mg)_2Si_4O_{10}(OH)_2 \cdot nH_2O$.

- **Reactivity**: Chemically inert under normal conditions. Exhibits cation exchange properties and can adsorb ions and organic molecules.
- **Stability**: Stable under normal conditions; swells in the presence of water, forming a thixotropic gel.

Storage:

- **Conditions**: Store in a cool, dry place in tightly closed containers to prevent moisture absorption and contamination.
- **Precautions**: Protect from prolonged exposure to moisture. Use appropriate personal protective equipment (PPE) to avoid inhalation of dust.

Uses:

1. **Medical**:
   - **Topical Applications**: Used in creams and ointments for its soothing and absorptive properties.
   - **Internal Use**: Occasionally used in detoxification protocols due to its adsorptive properties, though this is less common.

2. **Cosmetics**:
   - **Face Masks and Cleansers**: Used for its ability to absorb excess oil and impurities from the skin.

3. **Industrial**:
   - **Drilling Mud**: Utilized in oil and gas drilling to lubricate the drill bit, remove cuttings, and stabilize boreholes.
   - **Foundry Sands**: Acts as a binder in molding sands for metal casting.
   - **Water Treatment**: Used to clarify and purify water by adsorbing impurities and heavy metals.
   - **Construction**: Employed in construction as a waterproofing and sealing agent, particularly in geotechnical and environmental applications.

4. **Agriculture**:
    - o **Soil Conditioner**: Improves soil structure and water retention.
    - o **Pesticide Carrier**: Used as a carrier for pesticides and fertilizers to improve their application and effectiveness.

Official Preparation: Bentonite Magma USP

- **Formulation**: A suspension of bentonite in purified water, used as a suspending agent in various pharmaceutical preparations.
- **Usage**: Employed as a stabilizing agent in liquid formulations to ensure even distribution of active ingredients.
- **Dosage**: The specific dosage depends on the formulation in which it is used.
- **Administration**: Typically used in compounding pharmacies for preparing suspensions and emulsions.

Storage of Official Preparations:

- **Conditions**: Store at room temperature in a tightly closed container.
- **Precautions**: Shake well before use to ensure proper dispersion. Follow expiration dates and usage instructions.

Safety Information:

- **Side Effects**: Generally well-tolerated. Possible side effects when used topically include skin irritation or allergic reactions. Inhalation of dust should be avoided to prevent respiratory issues.
- **Contraindications**: Not recommended for individuals with known hypersensitivity to bentonite.
- **Interactions**: Inform healthcare providers of all medications being taken, as bentonite can adsorb and reduce the effectiveness of certain drugs when used internally.

CHAPTER – 12

ANTIMICROBIAL AGENTS – I

Mr. Abu Tahir

Assistant Professor, Rajiv Gandhi Institute of Pharmacy, Faculty of
Pharmaceutical Science & Technology, AKS University Satna, MP-India

ABSTRACT:

Antimicrobial agents are substances used to kill or inhibit the growth of microorganisms, including bacteria, viruses, fungi, and parasites. These agents play a crucial role in preventing and treating infections, maintaining hygiene, and preserving food and other perishable products. Antimicrobial agents can be classified into several categories based on their target organisms and mechanisms of action, such as antibiotics, antivirals, antifungals, and antiparasitics. Antibiotics like penicillin and tetracycline target bacterial infections by disrupting cell wall synthesis or protein production, while antifungals like fluconazole inhibit fungal cell membrane synthesis. Antivirals such as acyclovir interfere with viral replication processes, and antiparasitics like ivermectin combat parasitic infections. The development and use of antimicrobial agents have revolutionized medicine, significantly reducing mortality and morbidity associated with infectious diseases. However, the overuse and misuse of these agents have led to the emergence of antimicrobial resistance (AMR), a major global health concern. AMR occurs when microorganisms evolve mechanisms to resist the effects of antimicrobials, rendering standard treatments ineffective. To combat this issue, it is essential to use antimicrobial agents judiciously, follow prescribed treatments accurately, and invest in research for new antimicrobials and alternative therapies. Antimicrobial stewardship programs aim to optimize the use of these agents, ensuring their efficacy for future generations while minimizing the risk of resistance development.

Definition: An antimicrobial is an agent that kills microorganisms or stops their growth.

Mechanism of action of Antimicrobial drug fall into 5 basic categories:

The most common targets for antimicrobial drug actions fall into 5 basic categories:

1. Inhibition of cell wall synthesis
2. Inhibition of protein synthesis
3. Inhibition of nucleic acid synthesis
4. Effects on cell membrane sterols (antifungal agents)
5. Inhibition of unique metabolic steps

Ideal requirements of antiseptics and disinfectants:

a. Should have a high activity
b. It must have a broad spectrum of action
c. Onset of action fast.
d. It must have a broad spectrum of action.
e. Lack of local irritant or allergic effects on tissues.
f. Low toxicity
g. It must be chemically resistant.
h. It should have a high activity.
i. High availability and low cost.

CONTROL OF MICROBIAL GROWTH:

1. Sterilizing Agents:
2. Disinfectants: They are antimicrobial agents that are applied to the surface of non-living objects to destroy microorganisms that are living on the objects. Disinfection does not necessarily kill all microorganisms, especially resistant bacterial spores; it is less effective than sterilization.

3. Antiseptics (from Greek anti: "against" and sēptikos: "putrefactive"): They are antimicrobial substances that are applied to living tissue/skin to reduce the possibility of infection, sepsis, or putrefaction.

4. Chemotherapeutics: The chemical agents which is used in the clinical application of antimicrobial agents to treat infectious disease

Classification of Antiseptics and Disinfectants:

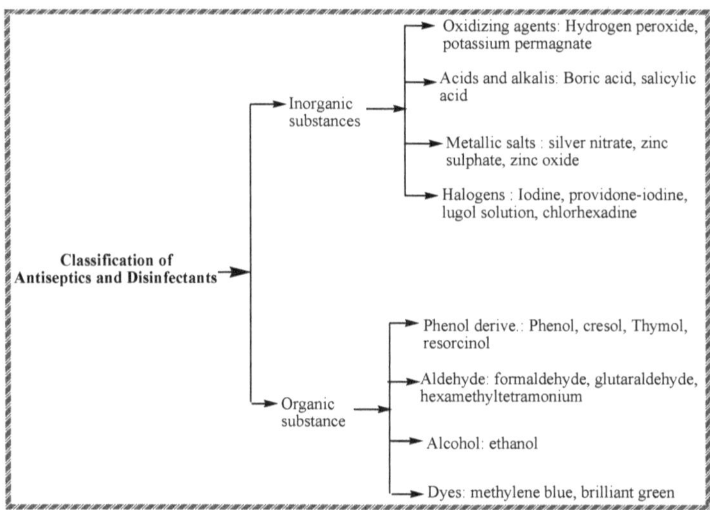

POTASSIUM PERMAGNATE

Chemical formula: $KMnO_4$ **Mol. Formula: 1588.03**

Physical Properties:

1. **Appearance**: Dark purple or almost black crystalline solid.

2. **Odor**: Odorless.

3. **Melting Point**: Decomposes at about 240°C.

4. **Solubility**: Soluble in water, giving a deep purple solution; slightly soluble in acetone.

5. **Density**: 2.703 g/cm³.

6. **Molecular Weight**: 158.04 g/mol.

Chemical Properties:

1. **Oxidizing Agent**: Potassium permanganate is a strong oxidizing agent, capable of reacting with various organic and inorganic substances.
2. **Stability**: Stable under normal conditions but decomposes on heating, releasing oxygen.
3. **Reactivity**: Reacts with reducing agents, acids, and organic compounds.
4. **Decomposition**: When heated, it decomposes to potassium manganate (K_2MnO_4), manganese dioxide (MnO_2), and oxygen (O_2).
5. **Redox Reactions**: In acidic conditions, it reduces to manganese(II) ion (Mn^{2+}), and in neutral or alkaline conditions, it reduces to manganese dioxide (MnO_2).

Preparation:

1. **Industrial Production**: Potassium permanganate is produced industrially from manganese dioxide (MnO_2) in a process involving the oxidation of MnO_2 with potassium hydroxide (KOH) and a source of oxygen (such as air or a chemical oxidant) at high temperatures to form potassium manganate (K_2MnO_4), which is then electrolytically oxidized to potassium permanganate ($KMnO_4$).
   - **Step 1**: $2MnO_2 + 4KOH + O_2 \rightarrow 2K_2MnO_4 + 2H_2O$
   - **Step 2**: $K_2MnO4 + Cl_2 \rightarrow 2KMnO_4 + 2KCl$

Storage:

1. **Container**: Store in a tightly closed container.
2. **Environment**: Store in a cool, dry, well-ventilated area away from incompatible substances (such as reducing agents and organic materials).
3. **Protection**: Protect from moisture, heat, and direct sunlight.

Tests:

1. **Purity Test**: Assay of potassium permanganate is typically done by titration with a reducing agent such as sodium oxalate or ferrous ammonium sulfate.
2. **Identity Test**: Confirmatory tests include reaction with sulfuric acid to produce a green solution (MnO_4^{2-}) and with reducing agents to observe color change from purple to colorless.
3. **Contaminants**: Tests for impurities such as chlorides, sulfates, and heavy metals may also be performed.

Uses:

1. **Antiseptic**: Used in dilute solutions as an antiseptic for treating wounds, dermatitis, and fungal infections.
2. **Water Treatment**: Used in water treatment for removing iron, hydrogen sulfide, and other contaminants.
3. **Oxidation Reactions**: Employed in organic chemistry for the oxidation of various organic compounds.
4. **Analytical Chemistry**: Used as an analytical reagent in redox titrations.
5. **Waste Treatment**: Utilized in wastewater treatment to remove organic contaminants and odors.

Official Preparations:

1. **Topical Solutions**: Dilute solutions of potassium permanganate are used for medical purposes, such as the treatment of infected eczema or dermatitis.
2. **Permanganate Tablets**: Tablets that can be dissolved in water to prepare antiseptic solutions.

BORIC ACID

Chemical formula: H_3BO_3 **Molecular weight**: 61.83

Synonyms: Boracic acid, Orthoboric acid

Physical Properties:

- **Appearance**: White crystalline powder or colorless crystals.
- **Molecular Weight**: 61.83 g/mol.
- **Melting Point**: 170.9 °C (decomposes).
- **Solubility**: Soluble in water (4.7 g/100 mL at 20 °C), alcohol, glycerin, and other solvents.
- **Density**: 1.435 g/cm³.
- **Odor and Taste**: Odorless with a slightly bitter taste.

Preparation: Boric acid can be prepared through the reaction of borax (sodium tetraborate decahydrate, $Na_2B_4O_7 \cdot 10H_2O$) with a mineral acid like hydrochloric acid (HCl):

$$Na_2B_4O_7 + 2HCl + 5H_2O \rightarrow 4H_3BO_3 + 2NaCl$$

The boric acid is then filtered, washed, and dried.

Chemical Properties:

- **Chemical Formula**: H_3BO_3.
- **Reactivity**: Weak acid with mild antiseptic properties. Reacts with bases to form borates.
- **Stability**: Stable under normal conditions; decomposes at high temperatures to form boron trioxide (B_2O_3) and water.

Storage:

- **Conditions**: Store in a tightly closed container in a cool, dry place.
- **Precautions**: Protect from moisture and contamination.

Qualitative Tests for Boric Acid:

1. **Turmeric Paper Test:**
   - **Materials**: Turmeric paper (or turmeric powder), hydrochloric acid (HCl), and boric acid sample.

- o **Procedure**:
    1. Moisten a strip of turmeric paper with the boric acid solution.
    2. Allow the paper to dry.
    3. Dip the dried paper in a solution of hydrochloric acid.
    4. **Observation**: A red or brownish-red color indicates the presence of boric acid.
  - o **Explanation**: Boric acid reacts with the turmeric to form a red complex (rosocyanine) in an acidic medium.

2. **Flame Test**:
   - o **Materials**: Platinum wire, boric acid sample, and a Bunsen burner.
   - o **Procedure**:
     1. Dip a platinum wire into the boric acid sample.
     2. Hold the wire in the flame of a Bunsen burner.
     3. **Observation**: A green flame indicates the presence of boric acid.
   - o **Explanation**: Boric acid produces a characteristic green flame when heated, due to the formation of volatile boron compounds.

3. **Glycerol Test**:
   - o **Materials**: Glycerol, sulfuric acid (H_2SO_4), and boric acid sample.
   - o **Procedure**:
     1. Mix a small amount of boric acid with glycerol.
     2. Add a few drops of concentrated sulfuric acid.
     3. Heat the mixture gently.
     4. **Observation**: A green flame upon ignition indicates the presence of boric acid.
   - o **Explanation**: The reaction between boric acid and glycerol in the presence of sulfuric acid forms a boric ester, which burns with a green flame.

Quantitative Tests for Boric Acid:

1. **Titration with Sodium Hydroxide (NaOH):**
   - **Materials**: Sodium hydroxide (NaOH) solution, phenolphthalein indicator, and boric acid sample.
   - **Procedure**:
     1. Dissolve a known amount of boric acid in water.
     2. Add a few drops of phenolphthalein indicator.
     3. Titrate with a standard NaOH solution until a persistent pink color appears.
     4. **Calculation**: Use the volume of NaOH solution used to calculate the concentration of boric acid.
   - **Explanation**: Boric acid reacts with NaOH to form borate ions and water, and the endpoint is indicated by the phenolphthalein turning pink.

General Preparation of Reagents:

- **Turmeric Paper**: Prepare by soaking filter paper in a turmeric solution (turmeric dissolved in ethanol or water), then drying it.
- **Sodium Hydroxide Solution**: Prepare a standard NaOH solution by dissolving a known amount of NaOH in distilled water and standardizing it against a primary standard such as potassium hydrogen phthalate (KHP).

Uses:

1. **Medical**:
   - **Antiseptic**: Used in topical applications to prevent infections in minor cuts and burns.
   - **Ophthalmic Solutions**: Used as an eye wash to relieve irritation.
2. **Industrial**:
   - **Insecticide**: Effective against ants and cockroaches.
   - **Flame Retardant**: Used in textiles and paper products.

3. **Cosmetics**: Used in powders and creams for its mild antiseptic properties.

4. **Laboratory**: Used as a buffer solution component.

Official Preparation: Boric Acid Ophthalmic Solution USP

- **Formulation**: Typically available in 2% to 4% aqueous solutions.

- **Usage**: Used as an eye wash to relieve irritation and cleanse the eyes.

- **Dosage**: Administered as directed, usually a few drops in the affected eye several times a day.

- **Administration**: For topical ophthalmic use only.

Storage of Official Preparations:

- **Conditions**: Store at room temperature in a tightly closed container.

- **Precautions**: Keep out of reach of children and avoid contamination.

CHAPTER – 13

ANTIMICROBIAL AGENTS – II

Ms. Shikha Singh

Assistant Professor, Rajiv Gandhi Institute of Pharmacy, Faculty of

Pharmaceutical Science & Technology, AKS University Satna, MP-India

---

ABSTRACT:

Hydrogen peroxide is a pale blue liquid in its pure form and appears colorless when diluted. It is known for its strong oxidizing properties, making it a powerful bleaching agent. Commonly used as a disinfectant and antiseptic, hydrogen peroxide decomposes into water and oxygen, a reaction catalyzed by light and certain enzymes. This decomposition releases oxygen, making it useful in treating wounds as it helps kill bacteria by oxidation. In industry, it is used for bleaching textiles and paper. Concentrated solutions are used as rocket propellants. However, it must be stored in dark, tightly sealed containers to prevent decomposition. Its applications extend to environmental management, where it is used to treat wastewater. Safety precautions are necessary due to its corrosive nature, particularly in higher concentrations. It is also employed in cosmetic formulations, such as hair bleaches and tooth-whitening products. Chlorinated lime, also known as bleaching powder, is a white or grayish-white powder with a strong chlorine odor. It is primarily used as a disinfectant and bleaching agent due to its high chlorine content. When dissolved in water, it releases hypochlorous acid, a potent disinfectant effective against a broad spectrum of pathogens. Chlorinated lime is used extensively in sanitation, water treatment, and for disinfecting drinking water in emergencies. In the textile industry, it is employed for bleaching fabrics and paper. It must be stored in airtight containers to prevent the loss of chlorine and degradation of its disinfectant properties. The compound is also used in agriculture to disinfect animal housing and control odors. Safety measures are important, as it can cause irritation to the skin, eyes, and respiratory system. Iodine is a dark gray or purple-black solid with a metallic luster and characteristic odor. It sublimates easily at room temperature, forming a violet gas. Iodine is an essential micronutrient necessary for the production of thyroid hormones. It is widely used in medicine as an antiseptic for treating wounds and as a disinfectant. Iodine solutions, such as tincture of iodine and povidone-iodine, are applied to disinfect skin before surgery. It is also used in the production of iodine compounds for pharmaceuticals and as a catalyst in various chemical reactions. Iodine is crucial in analytical chemistry for iodometric titrations. In nutrition, iodized salt helps prevent iodine deficiency disorders. Storage requires dark, well-sealed containers to prevent sublimation and degradation. Safety considerations include avoiding prolonged exposure to iodine vapors, which can be irritating to the eyes and respiratory tract.

HYDROGEN PEROXIDE

Chemical formula: H_2O_2 **Mol.Wt:** 34.016

Preparation of Hydrogen peroxide:

1. When barium peroxide reacts with sulphuric acid gives hydrogen peroxide.

$$BaO_2 + H_2SO_4 \longrightarrow BaSO_4 + H_2O_2$$

2. It is prepared by the reaction of barium peroxide with phosphoric acid.

$$3BaO_2 + 2H_3PO_4 \longrightarrow Ba_3(PO_4)_3 + H_2O_2$$

3. It may be also prepared by by treating sodium peroxide with dilute sulphuric acid at a low temperature.

$$Na_2O_2 + H_2SO_4 \longrightarrow Na_2SO_4 + H_2O_2$$

4. When hydrated barium peroxide is stirred strongly into ice-cooled water in a stream of calcium dioxide, it gives hydrogen peroxide.

$$BaO_2 + CO_2 + H_2O \longrightarrow CaCO_3 \downarrow + H_2O_2$$

5. It is also produced by electrolyte process. Sulphuric acid on electrolysis gives persulphuric acid that on vacuum distillation gives hydrogen peroxide.

$$2H_2SO_4 \longrightarrow H_2S_2O_8 + H_2$$

Persulphuric acid

$$H_2S_3O_8 \longrightarrow 2H_2SO_4 + H_2O_2$$

Physical Properties:

- **Appearance**: Colorless liquid.
- **Molecular Weight**: 34.01 g/mol.
- **Melting Point**: -0.43 °C.
- **Boiling Point**: 150.2 °C (decomposes).
- **Solubility**: Miscible with water and alcohol.
- **Density**: 1.45 g/cm³ (for 30% solution).
- **Odor and Taste**: Slightly sharp, characteristic odor.

Chemical Properties:

- **Chemical Formula**: H_2O_2.
- **Reactivity**: Strong oxidizing agent. Decomposes exothermically to form water and oxygen.

$$2H_2O_2 \rightarrow 2H_2O + O_2$$

- **Stability**: Decomposes over time, especially when exposed to light, heat, or contaminants.

Storage:

- **Conditions**: Store in a cool, dark place in a tightly closed, opaque container.

- **Precautions**: Avoid exposure to light, heat, and contaminants. Store away from flammable materials.

Uses:

1. **Medical**:
   - **Antiseptic**: Used to clean wounds and prevent infection.
   - **Oral Care**: Used in mouthwashes and toothpaste for its antibacterial properties.
2. **Industrial**:
   - **Bleaching Agent**: Used in paper and textile industries.
   - **Disinfectant**: Used to sanitize surfaces and equipment.
3. **Household**:
   - **Cleaning Agent**: Used for general disinfection and stain removal.
4. **Laboratory**: Used in various analytical and preparative chemistry applications.

Official Preparation: Hydrogen Peroxide Solution USP

- **Formulation**: Commonly available in concentrations ranging from 3% to 6%.
- **Usage**: Used as an antiseptic for minor cuts and abrasions, as well as a mouth rinse.
- **Dosage**: For wound cleaning, apply directly to the affected area. For mouth rinse, dilute with water before use.
- **Administration**: Topical application or diluted for oral use.

Storage of Official Preparations:

- **Conditions**: Store at room temperature in a tightly closed, light-resistant container.
- **Precautions**: Keep out of reach of children and avoid contact with eyes.

CHLORINATED LIME

Chemical formula: $Ca(OCl)Cl$ **Molecular weight:** 136.98

Synonyms: Bleaching powder, chloride of lime.

Bleaching powder is not a simple mixture of calcium hypochlorite, calcium chloride, and calcium hydroxide. Instead, it is a mixture consisting principally of calcium hypochlorite [$Ca(OCl)_2$], dibasic calcium hypochlorite[$Ca_3(OCl)_2(OH)_4$], and dibasic calcium chloride [$Ca_3Cl_2(OH)_4$]. It is made from slightly moist slaked lime.

Physical Properties:

1. **Appearance**: White or grayish-white granular powder.
2. **Odor**: Strong chlorine smell.
3. **Solubility**: Moderately soluble in water, forming a slightly cloudy solution; insoluble in alcohol.
4. **Density**: Approximately 2.35 g/cm³.
5. **Molecular Weight**: 142.98 g/mol.
6. **Melting Point**: Decomposes before melting at temperatures above 100°C.
7. **pH**: Alkaline, with a pH around 11 when dissolved in water.

Chemical Properties:
Preparation:

1. **Industrial Production**:
   - Produced by the chlorination of lime (calcium hydroxide, $Ca(OH)_2$).
   - **Reaction**: $2Ca(OH)_2 + 2Cl_2 \rightarrow Ca(OCl)_2 + CaCl_2 + 2H_2O_2$
   - The resulting product contains a mixture of calcium hypochlorite, calcium chloride, and calcium hydroxide.

Storage:

1. **Container**: Store in tightly sealed, non-metallic containers.

2. **Environment**: Store in a cool, dry, and well-ventilated area away from organic materials, acids, and combustible substances.
3. **Protection**: Keep away from moisture, heat, and direct sunlight to prevent decomposition and loss of chlorine content.

Tests:

1. **Assay for Available Chlorine**:
   - Titration method using a reducing agent such as sodium thiosulfate.
   - **Procedure**:
     1. Dissolve a known quantity of chlorinated lime in water.
     2. Add potassium iodide and acidify with acetic acid.
     3. Titrate the liberated iodine with sodium thiosulfate using a starch indicator.
     4. Calculate the available chlorine content based on the volume of sodium thiosulfate used.
2. **Identity Test**:
   - Dissolve a small amount in water and add dilute hydrochloric acid.
   - **Observation**: Liberation of chlorine gas indicates the presence of hypochlorite.
3. **Impurities Test**:
   - Check for the presence of calcium chloride, calcium hydroxide, and other impurities by appropriate chemical analysis methods.

Chemical properties:

1. Calcium hypochlorite reacts with carbon dioxide to form calcium carbonate and release dichlorine monoxide:

$$Ca(ClO)_2 + CO_2 \rightarrow CaCO_3 + Cl_2O\uparrow$$

2. calcium hypochlorite reacts with hydrochloric acid to form calcium chloride, water and chlorine:

$$Ca(OCl)_2 + 4\ HCl \rightarrow CaCl_2 + 2\ H_2O + 2\ Cl_2$$

3. Treatment of chlorinated lime with dilute sulphuric acids liberates Hypochlorous acid which behaves as oxidizing and bleaching agents.

$$2\ Ca(OCl)_2 + 4\ H_2SO_4 \rightarrow CaCl_2 + CaSO_4 + 2HClO$$
$$HClO \rightarrow HCl + [O]$$

4. On treatment with excess of dilute acid or CO_2, the whole of chlorine is liberated:

$$Ca(OCl)_2 + H_2SO_4 \rightarrow CaSO_4 + H_2O + Cl_2$$

Assay:

1. **Principle:** Principle based on iodometric titration. An aqueous suspension of weighed quantity is treated with acetic acid in the presence of excess of potassium iodide. The reaction occurs:

$$Ca(OCl)Cl + 2CH_3COOH \longrightarrow Ca(CH_3COO)_2\ HCl + HOCl\ \text{(Hypochlorous acid)}$$

$$HOCl + HCl \longrightarrow H_2O + Cl_2$$

$$2KI + Cl_2 \longrightarrow 2KCl + I_2$$

Hypochlorous acid and hydrochloric acid react to form chlorine. The chlorine thus produced, displaces an equivalent amount of iodine from potassium iodide. The liberated iodine is treated with standard solution of sodium thiosulphate using mucilage of starch as an indicator. The end point is disappearance of blue colour.

$$2Na_2S_2O_3 + I_2 \longrightarrow Na_2S_4O_6 + 2NaI$$
$$\text{Sodium tetrathionate}$$

2. **Procedure:** Weigh accurately 4.0 g of chlorinated lime and triturate it in a glass-pestle-mortar with a little DW. Transfer the paste quantitatively into a 1 litre volumetric flask and shake thoroughly. Take a 100 ml volumetric flask, rinse it with a small quantity of the suspension from the 1 litre flask and finally fill it up with the suspension. Rinse out a 250 ml iodine flask containing a little dilute acetic acid and a little of the suspension from the 1-litre flask in order to oxidise any inorganic substance present in the iodine flask. Finally, wash it thoroughly with distilled water. Now, transfer 100 ml of the suspension completely from the 100 ml volumetric flask to the iodine flask by washing the former repeatedly with distilled water. Add to it acetic acid 5 ml followed by KI 3.0 g and shake the contents of the flask thoroughly. Titrate the liberated iodine with 0.1 N sodium thiosulphate which is equivalent to 0.003546 g of chlorine.

Uses:

1. **Disinfectant:**
   - Used to disinfect drinking water, swimming pools, and wastewater.
   - Employed in sanitation and public health to control the spread of infectious diseases.

2. **Bleaching Agent:**
   - Utilized in the textile and paper industries for bleaching fabrics and pulp.

3. **Agriculture:**
   - Used to disinfect animal housing, equipment, and to control odors.

4. **Industrial Applications:**
   - Applied in chemical manufacturing processes that require strong oxidizing agents.

5. **Household Cleaner:**

o Included in various household cleaning products for disinfecting surfaces.

Official Preparations:

1. **Bleaching Powder (British Pharmacopoeia):**
   o Contains a defined amount of available chlorine, used as a standard disinfectant and bleaching agent.

2. **Commercial Disinfectants:**
   o Formulated with specified concentrations of calcium hypochlorite for use in water treatment and sanitation.

3. **Chlorinated Lime Solution:**
   o Prepared by dissolving a measured amount in water for specific disinfection purposes in healthcare and public health settings.

<h2 style="text-align:center">IODINE</h2>

Mol. Formula: I_2   **Mol. Wt: 253.8**

Physical Properties:

- Non-metallic
- Dark-gray/purple-black, lustrous, solid element.
- Odour: Strong, harsh odor
- It is volatile at room temperature and its vapour attack both cork and rubber.
- It is slightly soluble in water
- A gray solid that changes into purple vapors when heated
- Soluble in alcohol and dissolves freely in ether, chloroform and carbon disulphide.
- It melts at 114^0C.
- Iodine is the most electropositive halogen and the least reactive of the halogens even if it can still form compounds with many elements.

- Iodine sublime easily on heating to give a purple vapour

Preparation of Iodine:

1. From oil-field water: Oil-field water can be illustrated by oxidation of iodides in the water to inorganic iodine to the molecular form.

$$2NaI + 2NaNO_2 + 2H_2SO_4 = I_2 + 2Na_2SO_4 + 2NO2 + 2H_2O$$

2. Chile contains sodium nitrate and sodium iodate. During its crystallization, sodium nitrate separate out as crystals whereas sodium iodated remain in the mother liquor. Much iodine is obtained from this mother liquor by treatment with sodium hydrogen sulphate which results in the precipitation of iodine.

$$2NaIO_3 + 5NaHSO_3 = 2Na_2SO_3 + 3NaHSO_4 + I_2 + H_2O$$

Chemical Properties:

1. In aqueous medium Iodine behaves as an oxidizing agents

$$I_2 + H_2O = HI + HIO$$

2. Iodine reacts with liquor ammonia to yield a black explosive powder, nitrogen trioxide.

$$2NH_3 + 3I_2 = NI_3 + 3HI$$

3. With cold sodium hydroxide solution, iodine reacts to form a hypoiodide which hydrolyses to give hypoiodous acid.

$$2NaOH + I_2 = NaIO + H_2O = HIO + NaOH$$

Identification Tests:

1. When gently heated, it gives violet coloured vapours which are condensing forming a bluish-black crystalline sublimate.

2. With solution of potassium iodide and starch, a deep blue colour is produced which is disappears on boiling but reappears on cooling

Uses:

1. Iodine is used to treat and prevent iodine deficiency (Goitre)
2. As an antiseptic.
3. Iodide salts are used in pharmaceuticals and disinfectants, printing inks and dyes, catalysts, animal feed supplements and photographic chemicals.
4. For iodine deficiency it can be given by mouth or injection into a muscle.
5. It is an essential trace element of human diet
6. As an antiseptic it may be used on wounds that are wet or to disinfect the skin before surgery.

PROVIDONE-IODINE

It is a **water**-soluble iodophor (or iodine-releasing agent) that consists of a complex between iodine and a solubilizing polymer carrier, polyvinyl pyrrolidone.

Povidone-iodine is a chemical complex of povidone, hydrogen iodide, and elemental iodine. It is soluble in water forming a golden brown solution. In aqueous solution, a dynamic equilibrium occurs between free iodine (I_2), the active bactericidal agent, and the PVP-I-complex.

Physical Properties

- **Appearance**: Povidone-iodine is a reddish-brown liquid or powder.
- **Solubility**: It is soluble in water and alcohol, forming a clear solution.
- **Odor**: It has a slight iodine odor.
- **pH**: Aqueous solutions of povidone-iodine typically have a pH between 2.0 and 6.0.
- **Viscosity**: The viscosity of povidone-iodine solutions can vary based on the concentration and formulation.

Chemical Properties

- **Chemical Formula**: $(C_6H_9NO)_n \cdot xI_2$
- **Molecular Weight**: Variable due to its polymeric nature; typical molecular weights range from 20,000 to 70,000.
- **Stability**: Povidone-iodine is stable under normal storage conditions but can be decomposed by strong alkalis and reducing agents.
- **Complexation**: It is a complex of polyvinylpyrrolidone (PVP) and iodine, providing a slow release of iodine.

Preparation

Povidone-iodine is prepared by complexing iodine with polyvinylpyrrolidone (PVP). The process involves:

1. Dissolving PVP in water or alcohol.
2. Adding iodine to the PVP solution.
3. Stirring the mixture until a stable complex is formed.
4. Adjusting the concentration as needed for different formulations.

Testing

- **Iodine Content**: The iodine content is determined by titration methods, usually involving sodium thiosulfate.
- **pH Testing**: The pH of povidone-iodine solutions is measured using standard pH meters.
- **Microbial Effectiveness**: Testing for antimicrobial efficacy involves exposing microbial cultures to povidone-iodine and assessing the reduction in microbial count.
- **Stability Testing**: Stability tests include storing the product under various conditions and periodically testing its physical and chemical properties.

Uses

- **Surgical Antiseptic**: Used to disinfect the skin before and after surgery to prevent infections.

- **Wound Care**: Applied to minor cuts, abrasions, and burns to reduce the risk of infection.
- **Hand Sanitizer**: Used by healthcare professionals for hand disinfection.
- **Mucosal Antiseptic**: Used in diluted form for antiseptic irrigation and rinsing.
- **Infection Control**: Effective against a broad spectrum of pathogens, including bacteria, viruses, and fungi, making it a versatile antiseptic in various healthcare settings.

Official preparations:

1. Solutions
2. Cream

CHAPTER – 14

EXPECTORANTS

Mrs. Evneet Kaur Bhatia

Assistant Professor, Rajiv Gandhi Institute of Pharmacy, Faculty of

Pharmaceutical Science & Technology, AKS

ABSTRACT:

Expectorants are a class of drugs used to help clear mucus and phlegm from the respiratory tract. These medications are particularly beneficial for individuals suffering from respiratory conditions such as the common cold, bronchitis, and asthma, where mucus accumulation can obstruct airways and exacerbate symptoms. The primary mechanism of action for expectorants involves thinning the mucus, making it easier to expel through coughing. This is achieved by increasing the water content of the mucus, thereby reducing its viscosity. Guaifenesin is one of the most commonly used expectorants, available in many over-the-counter formulations. In addition to their use in treating acute respiratory infections, expectorants are also employed in managing chronic conditions like chronic obstructive pulmonary disease (COPD) and cystic fibrosis. For individuals with these chronic conditions, regular use of expectorants can significantly improve breathing and quality of life by maintaining clearer airways. While generally safe for most people, expectorants should be used with caution in individuals with certain medical conditions, such as heart disease or high blood pressure, due to potential side effects. The effectiveness of expectorants can vary depending on the individual's condition and the specific medication used. Some people may find that expectorants significantly relieve their symptoms, while others may experience only minimal benefits. It is important to use these medications as directed by a healthcare professional to avoid potential complications, such as overuse or interactions with other medications. Additionally, maintaining adequate hydration is crucial when taking expectorants, as this supports their mucus-thinning effects. Despite their widespread use, there is some debate in the medical community about the overall efficacy of expectorants. Some studies suggest that their benefits may be more pronounced in certain populations or when used in combination with other treatments, such as bronchodilators or antihistamines. However, many patients report subjective improvements in symptoms, which underscores the importance of considering individual responses to treatment. Natural remedies, such as steam inhalation, increased fluid intake, and herbal teas, are also popular methods for managing mucus build-up. These approaches can complement the use of expectorants and provide additional relief. Honey, for example, has been used traditionally to soothe the throat and may help in loosening mucus. It's important for patients to discuss these options with their healthcare providers to ensure they are appropriate and safe. The role of expectorants in pediatric care requires special consideration. While they can be effective in children, dosages need to be carefully managed, and not all formulations are suitable for young patients. Parents should always consult a pediatrician before administering expectorants to children to avoid adverse effects.

Introduction:

Expectorants are Drugs that help in removing sputum from the respiratory tract either by:- increasing the fluidity (or reducing the viscosity) of sputum OR increasing the volume of fluids that have to be expelled from the respiratory tract by coughing.

Classification of Expectorants:

According the mechanism of action:

1. Sedative expectorant
2. Stimulant expectorant

Sedative expectorant: These are stomach irritant expectorants which are able to produce their effect through stimulation of gastric reflexes. e.g. Inorganic Compounds – Antimony potassium tartrate, Ammonium chloride, Sodium citrate, Potassium iodide

Stimulant expectorant: These are the expectorants which bring about a stimulation of the secretory cells of the respiratory tract directly or indirectly. Since these drugs stimulate secretion, more fluid in respiratory tract and sputum is diluted.

POTASSIUM IODIDE

Mol. Formula: KI   **Mol. Wt.**: 166

Potassium iodide is a **metal-halide salt** featuring an **ionic bond between the potassium cation (K^+) and the iodide anion.**

Physical Properties of Potassium Iodide (KI)

1. **Appearance**: Potassium iodide typically appears as a white, crystalline powder or solid.

2. **Solubility**: It is highly soluble in water, with a solubility of approximately 140 grams per 100 milliliters at room temperature. It is also soluble in ethanol.

3. **Melting Point**: The melting point of potassium iodide is around 681 degrees Celsius (1,258 degrees Fahrenheit).

4. **Density**: The density of potassium iodide is approximately 3.13 grams per cubic centimeter.

5. **Taste**: It has a slightly bitter, salty taste.

Chemical Properties of Potassium Iodide

1. **Chemical Formula**: KI

2. **Molecular Weight**: The molecular weight of potassium iodide is approximately 166.00 grams per mole.

3. **Reactivity**: Potassium iodide is a relatively stable compound but can react with strong oxidizing agents. It can also undergo oxidation in the presence of light and moisture to form iodine and potassium iodate.

4. **Decomposition**: When heated to decomposition, it emits toxic fumes of iodine.

5. **Ionic Nature**: In aqueous solution, potassium iodide dissociates into potassium (K^+) and iodide (I^-) ions.

Preparation of Potassium Iodide

Potassium iodide can be prepared by several methods, including:

1. **Reaction of Potassium Hydroxide and Iodine**:

   $$6KOH+3I_2 \rightarrow 5KI+KIO_3+3H_2O$$

   The potassium iodate (KIO_3) formed can be separated and reduced to potassium iodide using a reducing agent like sulfur dioxide:

   $$2KIO_3+3SO_2+3H_2O \rightarrow 2KI+3H_2SO_4$$

2. **Direct Combination**: Another method involves the direct combination of potassium and iodine in a moist environment:

   $$2K+I2 \rightarrow 2KI2K + I$$

   $$2KI2K+I2 \rightarrow 2KI$$

Tests for Potassium Iodide

1. **Solubility Test**: Potassium iodide dissolves readily in water and ethanol, forming a clear solution.

2. **Reaction with Silver Nitrate**: When a solution of potassium iodide is treated with silver nitrate, a yellow precipitate of silver iodide (AgI) forms:

   $$KI+AgNO3 \rightarrow AgI+KNO_3KI + AgNO$$

   $$AKI+AgNO3 \rightarrow AgI+KNO_3$$

3. **Starch Test**: Potassium iodide can be tested with starch solution in the presence of an oxidizing agent. The iodide ions are oxidized to iodine, which forms a blue-black complex with starch.

Uses of Potassium Iodide

1. **Medical Use**: Potassium iodide is used in medicine to treat hyperthyroidism, as a thyroid blocking agent in radiation emergencies, and as an expectorant in cough medicines.

2. **Nutritional Supplement**: It is added to table salt to prevent iodine deficiency, known as iodized salt.

3. **Photography**: Potassium iodide is used in the preparation of photographic emulsions.

4. **Chemical Reagent**: It is employed in analytical chemistry as a reagent for iodometric titrations.

5. **Antiseptic**: Potassium iodide has antiseptic properties and is used in some disinfectants and antiseptic formulations.

6. **Animal Feeds**: It is added to animal feeds to ensure adequate iodine intake.

AMMONIUM CHLORIDE

Molecular formula: NH_4Cl **Mol. Weight:** 53.49

Ammonium Chloride contains not less than 99.0 per cent and not more than 100.5 per cent of NH_4Cl, calculated on the dried basis

Preparation:

1. Concentration of ammonia and hydrochloride solutions is added to two gas-washing bottles, respectively. Using pumps, air (action as gas-carrier) is injected in the gas washing tubes causing the streams of ammonia and hydrochloride in air to colloid and react giving the solid product, ammonium chloride.

2. It is product of the solvency process used to produce sodium carbonate.

$$CO_2 + 2NH_3 + 2NaCl + H_2O = 2NH_4Cl + Na_2CO_3$$

3. Ammonium chloride is prepared by combination of ammonia and hydrogen chloride gas.

$$NH_3 + HCl = NH_4Cl$$

4. Ammonium chloride is prepared by ammonium Sulphate with sodium chloride in equivalent proportions.

$$NH_3 + HCl \longrightarrow NH_4Cl$$

Physical Properties of Ammonium Chloride (NH_4Cl)

1. **Appearance**: Ammonium chloride appears as a white crystalline solid or powder.

2. **Solubility**: It is highly soluble in water, with a solubility of about 37 grams per 100 milliliters at 20 degrees Celsius. It is slightly soluble in ethanol and insoluble in acetone.

3. **Melting Point**: The melting point of ammonium chloride is approximately 338 degrees Celsius, but it sublimates (turns from solid to gas) at this temperature.

4. **Density**: The density of ammonium chloride is around 1.527 grams per cubic centimeter.

5. **Taste**: It has a salty, cooling taste.

Chemical Properties of Ammonium Chloride

1. **Chemical Formula**: NH_4Cl

2. **Molecular Weight**: The molecular weight of ammonium chloride is approximately 53.49 grams per mole.

3. **Acidic Nature**: In aqueous solution, ammonium chloride exhibits weak acidic properties because it partially dissociates into ammonium (NH_4^+) and chloride (Cl^-) ions. The ammonium ion can release a proton (H^+), making the solution slightly acidic.

4. **Reactivity**: Ammonium chloride reacts with strong bases like sodium hydroxide (NaOH) to produce ammonia gas (NH_3), water, and sodium chloride (NaCl):

$$NH_4Cl + NaOH \rightarrow NH_3 + H_2O + NaCl$$

$$NH_4Cl + NaOH \rightarrow NH3 + H_2O + NaCl$$

5. **Thermal Decomposition**: Upon heating, ammonium chloride decomposes into ammonia (NH_3) and hydrogen chloride (HCl) gases.

Preparation of Ammonium Chloride

Ammonium chloride can be prepared by several methods, including:

1. **Reaction of Ammonia and Hydrochloric Acid**:

$$NH_3 + HCl \rightarrow NH_4Cl$$

$$NH_4ClNH_3 + HCl \rightarrow NH_4Cl$$

   This is the most common industrial method, where ammonia gas is passed into hydrochloric acid, resulting in the formation of ammonium chloride.

2. **Double Decomposition Reaction**: By reacting ammonium sulfate with sodium chloride:

$$(NH_4)_2SO_4 + 2NaCl \rightarrow 2NH_4Cl + Na_2SO_4(NH_4)_2SO_4 + 2NaCl$$

Tests for Ammonium Chloride

1. **Solubility Test**: Ammonium chloride dissolves readily in water, forming a clear solution.

2. **Reaction with Strong Base**: When a solution of ammonium chloride is treated with a strong base like sodium hydroxide, ammonia gas is released, which can be identified by its characteristic pungent smell and by turning moist red litmus paper blue.

3. **Formation of White Smoke**: When exposed to concentrated hydrochloric acid fumes, ammonium chloride forms white smoke due to the formation of tiny solid

Assay:

1. The principle based on indirect acid base titration. An aqueous solution of ammonium chloride is treated with neutralized formaldehyde solution. After treatment, liberation of hydrochloric acid equivalent of ammonium chloride. This is then titrated with standard solution of sodium hydroxide using phenolphthalein as an indicator yielding pink colour at the end point.

$$4NH_4Cl + 4H_2O \longrightarrow 4NH_4OH + 4HCl$$

$$4NH_4OH + 6HCHO \longrightarrow (CH_2)_6N_4 + 10H_2O$$

Hexamine

$$4HCl + 4NaOH \longrightarrow 4NaCl + 4H_2O$$

Weigh accurately about 0.1 g, dissolve in 20 ml of *water* and add a mixture of 5 ml of *formaldehyde solution*, previously neutralised to *dilute phenolphthalein solution*, and 20 ml of *water*. After 2 minutes, titrate slowly with *0.1 M sodium hydroxide* using a further 0.2 ml of *dilute phenolphthalein solution* as indicator.

1 ml of *0.1 M sodium hydroxide* is equivalent to 0.005349 g of NH_4Cl.

2. Modified volhard's method of ammonium chloride. Sample of ammonium chloride is acidified with nitric acid in a titration flask and added a known excess quantity of standard solution of silver nitrate and nitrobenzene. Some of the silver nitrate is consumed due to its reaction with ammonium chloride. The remaining i.e. the unreacted silver nitrate is then determined by titration with a standard solution of ammonium thiocyanate using ferric alum (ferric ammonium sulphate) as an indicator.

$$NH_4Cl + AgNO_3 \longrightarrow AgCl + NH_4NO_3$$

(Excess)   (precipitate)

$$AgNO_3 + NH_4SCN \longrightarrow AgSCN + NH_4NO_3$$

(Unreacted)

$$3NH_4SCN + Fe^{3+} \longrightarrow Fe(SCN)_3 + 3NH_4^+$$

(Brick red color)
Ferric thiocyanate

1000 ml of 0.1N silver nitrate are equivalent to 1/10 NH_4Cl

Uses of Ammonium Chloride

1. **Medical Use**: Ammonium chloride is used as an expectorant in cough medicine, helping to clear mucus from the respiratory tract. It is also used to acidify urine in certain medical conditions.

2. **Fertilizer**: It serves as a nitrogen source in fertilizers, particularly for crops like rice and wheat.

3. **Industrial Use**: In the textile and leather industries, ammonium chloride is used in dyeing, tanning, and printing processes.

4. **Electroplating**: It is used in electroplating processes to improve the adhesion of the metal coating.

5. **Laboratory Reagent**: Ammonium chloride is used as a reagent in various laboratory analyses and experiments.

6. **Batteries**: It is used as an electrolyte in dry cell batteries, such as zinc-carbon batteries.

7. **Food Additive**: In some countries, ammonium chloride is used as a food additive, particularly in certain licorice candies to provide a salty flavor.

CHAPTER – 15

EMETICS

Mrs. Neha Soni

Assistant Professor, Rajiv Gandhi Institute of Pharmacy, Faculty of Pharmaceutical Science & Technology, AKS University Satna, MP-India

ABSTRACT:

Emetics are substances used to induce vomiting, typically in cases of poisoning or drug overdose to expel the toxic substance from the stomach. They have been used since ancient times for their therapeutic effects in clearing the digestive tract. One of the most well-known emetics is ipecac syrup, derived from the roots of the ipecacuanha plant. Emetics work by irritating the stomach lining or stimulating the chemoreceptor trigger zone (CTZ) in the brain, which in turn activates the vomiting center. While effective, their use is now limited due to potential complications, such as aspiration of vomit or damage to the esophagus. In modern medical practice, emetics are generally reserved for specific cases where the benefits outweigh the risks, and under the supervision of healthcare professionals. Activated charcoal and gastric lavage have largely replaced emetics for managing poisoning, as they are safer and more effective. However, emetics still hold a place in certain emergency protocols, especially when rapid intervention is required, and other methods are not readily available. The use of emetics requires careful consideration of the type of ingested substance. For instance, emetics are contraindicated in cases of ingestion of caustic agents, hydrocarbons, or when the patient is unconscious or has a compromised airway. Inappropriate use can lead to severe complications, emphasizing the need for professional guidance. Emetics are also found in veterinary medicine, where they are used to treat animals that have ingested harmful substances. Despite their limited use, emetics are a critical component of toxicology and emergency medicine. Research continues to explore safer and more effective methods to induce vomiting when necessary, reflecting the ongoing evolution of medical practices. Understanding the indications, mechanisms, and risks associated with emetics is essential for healthcare providers to make informed decisions in managing acute poisoning cases. Their historical and contemporary roles highlight the balance between therapeutic benefits and potential hazards in medical interventions.

Introduction:

These are the drugs which give rise to forced regurgitation (emesis) by which the contents of the stomach get expelled through the oral cavity.

Type of emetics: On the basis of mechanism of action

1. Locally acting emetics: by local irritation of gastric mucosa. e.g. Ammonium bicarbonate, Ipecacuanha
2. Centrally acting emetics: directly on the Chemoreceptor Trigger Zone (CTZ) in the floor of IV th ventricle in medulla e.g. Apomorphine & Morphine

Uses of emetics:

Vomiting is primarily considered to be a respiratory function, its ultimate result would cause the evacuation of the stomach thus emetics produces a reflux action by which TOXIC substances gets expelled in case of poisoning. Emetics are sometimes added to cough preparations in low doses to stimulate flow of respiratory tract secretions.

COPPER SULPHATE

Molecular formula: $CuSO_4$ **Mol. wt.:** 159.6

Physical Properties

1. **Appearance**: Copper sulphate appears as bright blue crystals or powder.
2. **Solubility**: It is highly soluble in water, with a solubility of approximately 31.6 grams per 100 milliliters at 20 degrees Celsius.

3. **Melting Point**: Copper sulphate pentahydrate ($CuSO_4 \cdot 5H_2O$) loses water molecules upon heating and turns white at around 150 degrees Celsius. The anhydrous form has a melting point of 1100 degrees Celsius.

4. **Density**: The density of copper sulphate pentahydrate is around 2.284 grams per cubic centimeter.

5. **Odor**: It is odorless.

Chemical Properties

1. **Chemical Formula**: $CuSO_4$

2. **Molecular Weight**: The molecular weight of copper sulphate pentahydrate is approximately 249.68 grams per mole.

3. **Reactivity**: Copper sulphate reacts with alkalis to form copper hydroxide and with reducing agents like iron to produce metallic copper.

4. **Dehydration**: Heating copper sulphate pentahydrate removes its water of crystallization, turning it into anhydrous copper sulphate (white powder).

Preparation

Copper sulphate can be prepared by reacting copper oxide or copper carbonate with sulfuric acid:

$$CuO + H_2SO4 \rightarrow CuSO_4 + H_2O$$
$$CuCO_3 + H_2SO_4 \rightarrow CuSO_4 + CO_2 + H_2O$$

Tests

1. **Flame Test**: Copper sulphate imparts a green color to the flame.

2. **Reaction with Sodium Hydroxide**: Forms a blue precipitate of copper hydroxide. $CuSO_4 + 2NaOH \rightarrow Cu(OH)_2 + Na_2SO_4$
$$4CuSO_4 + 2NaOH \rightarrow Cu(OH)_2 + Na_2SO_4$$

Assay:

It method is iodometric. Its assay is bases on the reaction between copper sulphate and potassium iodide in the presence of acetic acid.

$$CuSO_4 + 2KI \longrightarrow CuI_2 + K_2SO_4$$
$$\text{Cupric iodide}$$

Cupric iodide thus formed is unstable and decomposes into cuprous iodide and iodine according to the following equation:

$$2CuI_2 \rightleftharpoons Cu_2I_2 + I_2$$

Cupric iodide   cuprous iodide
(unstable)

Decomposition of cupric iodide into cuprous iodide and iodine is reversible. Potassium thiocyanider is added to check this reversible reaction by forming cuprous thiocyanide as follows:

$$Cu_2I_2 + 2KSCN \longrightarrow 2CuSCN + 2KI$$

The liberated iodine is titrated with a standard solution of sodium thiosulphate using starch solution (starch mucilage) as an indicator.

$$2Na_2S_2O_3 + I_2 \longrightarrow Na_2S_4O_6 + 2NaI$$

Sodium thiosuphate   sodium
tetrathionate

Uses

1. **Agriculture**: As a fungicide and herbicide.
2. **Electroplating**: Used in electroplating baths.
3. **Chemistry**: As a reagent in Fehling's solution and Benedict's solution for sugar tests.
4. **Dyes**: Used in the textile industry as a mordant.
5. **Medical**: Used as an astringent and antiseptic.

SODIUM POTASSIUM TARTRATE

Mol. Formula: $C_4H_4KNaO_6.4H_2O$ **Mol. Wt:** 283.23

Synonyms: Rochelle salt, Seignette's salt.

Physical Properties

1. **Appearance**: Sodium potassium tartrate appears as colorless or white crystals.
2. **Solubility**: It is soluble in water and insoluble in alcohol.
3. **Melting Point**: It has a melting point of around 70 degrees Celsius (decomposes).
4. **Density**: The density is approximately 1.79 grams per cubic centimeter.
5. **Odor**: It is odorless.

Chemical properties:

1. It gives characteristics reactions of sodium. Potassium and tartrate.
2. When heated it melts at 740C, when further heated it carbonizes and give off inflammable vapour having the odour of burnt sugar, with residue of potassium and sodium carbonates.

$$2C_4H_4O_6KNa + 5O_2 \longrightarrow K_2CO_3 + Na_2CO_3 + 4H_2O\uparrow + 6CO_2\uparrow$$

3. When equal volume of acetic acid is added to 5% solution of salt, a white crystalline precipitate of potassium bitartrate is obtained after 15 minutes.

Preparation

Sodium potassium tartrate can be prepared by neutralizing tartaric acid with a mixture of sodium carbonate and potassium carbonate:

$$H_2C_4H4O_6 + Na2CO_3 + K_2CO_3 \rightarrow 2KNaC_4H_4O_6 + 2H_2O + 2CO_2$$

$$2H_2C_4H4O6 + Na_2CO_3 + K_2CO_3 \rightarrow 2KNaC_4H_4O_6 + 2H_2O + 2CO_2$$

Tests

1. **Solubility Test**: It dissolves readily in water, forming a clear solution.

2. **Chemical Test**: When mixed with copper sulfate solution and heated, it forms a blue complex used in Fehling's test for reducing sugars.

Uses

1. **Chemistry**: As a primary ingredient in Fehling's solution and Benedict's solution for testing reducing sugars.
2. **Medicine**: Used as a laxative.
3. **Food Industry**: Used as a stabilizer and acidity regulator.
4. **Electroplating**: Acts as a complexing agent.
5. **Buffer Solutions**: Used in biochemical laboratories as a buffering agent.

CHAPTER – 16

HAEMATINICS

Mrs. Priyanka Soni

Assistant Professor, Rajiv Gandhi Institute of Pharmacy, Faculty of

Pharmaceutical Science & Technology, AKS University Satna, MP-India

ABSTRACT:

Haematinics are a class of medications and nutrients essential for the formation of blood and treating anemia. They primarily include iron, vitamin B12, and folic acid, which are crucial for the synthesis of hemoglobin and the maturation of red blood cells. Haematinics are prescribed to individuals with iron-deficiency anemia, megaloblastic anemia, and chronic diseases that affect blood production. These supplements can be administered orally or intravenously, depending on the severity of the deficiency and patient needs. Regular use of haematinics improves oxygen transport in the body, alleviating symptoms like fatigue, weakness, and shortness of breath. In addition to iron and vitamins, some haematinics contain other minerals such as copper and cobalt, which play supportive roles in hematopoiesis. Pregnant women often require haematinics to support increased blood volume and fetal development. The effectiveness of these supplements can be enhanced by dietary adjustments, such as increasing the intake of iron-rich foods like leafy greens, meat, and legumes. While generally safe, haematinics can cause side effects like gastrointestinal discomfort, and their use should be monitored by healthcare professionals to avoid complications like iron overload. Overall, haematinics are vital in managing and preventing various forms of anemia, contributing to improved health and quality of life.

Introduction:

Haematinics - a medicine that increases the hemoglobin content of the blood OR A hematinic is a nutrient required for the formation of blood cells in the process of hematopoiesis. The main Haematinics are iron, B12, and folate.

Anemia is a medical condition in which the red blood cell count or hemoglobin is less than normal. Anemia is caused by either a decrease in production of red blood cells or hemoglobin, or an increase in loss (usually due to bleeding) or destruction of red blood cells.

<h3 style="text-align:center">FERROUS SULPHATE</h3>

Molecular formula: $FeSo_4.7H_2O$

    Mol. Weight: 278.0

Synonyms: Green vitriol, Ferrosi sulfas.

Preparation:

1. Ferrous sulphate is prepared by adding a slight excess of iron to dilute sulphuric. When reaction slackens, the liquid is concentrated by boiling, filtered and allowed to cool. The crystal of ferrous sulphate are separated and dried at room temperature.

$$Fe + H_2SO_4 \longrightarrow FeSO_4 + H_2$$
$$\text{Ferrous sulpahte}$$

2. Ferrous sulphate is prepared by exposing moist iron pyrites to air when slow oxidation takes place.

$$2FeS_2 + 2H_2O + 7O_2 \longrightarrow 2FeSO_4 + 2H_2SO_4$$

3. Ferrous sulphate can be prepared by reacting iron with sulfuric acid:

$$Fe + H_2SO_4 \rightarrow FeSO_4 + H_2$$

It can also be produced as a byproduct of steel manufacturing or by the oxidation of pyrite (iron sulfide

Physical Properties

1. **Appearance**: Ferrous sulphate typically appears as blue-green crystals or a pale green powder.
2. **Solubility**: It is soluble in water, with a solubility of about 15 grams per 100 milliliters at room temperature. It is insoluble in ethanol.
3. **Melting Point**: The melting point of ferrous sulphate heptahydrate is approximately 64 degrees Celsius, after which it loses its water of crystallization.
4. **Density**: The density of ferrous sulphate heptahydrate is about 1.898 grams per cubic centimeter.
5. **Odor**: It is odorless.

Tests

1. **Iron Test**: When treated with potassium ferrocyanide, a blue precipitate of Prussian blue (iron(III) ferrocyanide) forms.
2. **Sulphate Test**: Adding barium chloride to a solution of ferrous sulphate produces a white precipitate of barium sulphate.

Chemical properties:

1. **Reactivity**: Ferrous sulphate can react with alkalis to form iron(II) hydroxide, which quickly oxidizes to iron(III) hydroxide in the presence of oxygen.
2. **Oxidation**: It oxidizes in moist air to form a brown coating of ferric sulphate ($Fe_2(SO_4)_3$).
3. **Hydration**: Ferrous sulphate exists in various hydrated forms, with the heptahydrate ($FeSO_4 \cdot 7H_2O$) being the most common.
4. Ferrous sulphate is heating, it decomposes into ferric oxide, sulphur dioxide and sulpher trioxide.

$$4FeSO_4 + 2H_2O + O_2 \longrightarrow 4Fe(OH)SO_4$$

5. Ferrous sulphate reacts with nitric acid form black coloured nitroso ferrous sulphate.

$$2FeSO_4 \longrightarrow Fe_2O_3 + SO_2 + SO_3$$

6. It decolourizes acidified potassium permagnate and turns acidified potassium dichromate green. Nitrogen dioxide is reduced to nitric oxide and black nitroso ferrous sulphate is formed.

Assay:

1. Titration is made with a standard solution of potassium permagnate in the presence of sulphuric acid. In this case potassium permagnate itself acts as indicator (self-indicator).

$$2KMnO_4 + 3H_2SO_4 \longrightarrow K_2SO_4 + 2MNSO_4 + 3H_2O + 5[O]$$

$$2FeSO_4 + H_2SO_4 + [O] \longrightarrow Fe_2(SO_4)_3 + H_2O \ ] X5$$

$$2KMnO_4 + 8H_2SO_4 + 10FeSo_4 \longrightarrow K_2SO_4 + 2MnSO_4 + 5Fe_2(SO_4)_3 + 8H_2O$$

A weigh quantity of sample is dissolved in water and dilute sulphuric acid in a titration flask. This is titrated with the standard solution of potassium permagnate till the appearance of permanent pink colour which is its end point.

2. It is based on oxidation- reduction titration. An acidified solution of the substance is titrated with ceric ammonium sulphate in the presence of sulphuric acd using ferroin sulphate solution as an indicator. Ceric ammonium sulphate is a strong oxidizing agent. It oxidizes the divalent ferrous sulphate to the trivalent ferric sulphate.

Ferrous sulphate + ceric salt $\longrightarrow$ Ferric sulpahte + Cerous salt

Take weigh 1 g of sample dissolved in 30 ml water and add 20 ml of dilute sulphuric acid, is titrated with 0.1 cerric ammonium sulphate using ferroin sulphate solution as indicator. Each ml of 0.1 N ceric ammonium sulphate is equivalent to 0.0278 g of $FeSO_4.7H_2O$.

Uses

1. **Medicine**: Used as an iron supplement to treat iron-deficiency anemia.
2. **Water Treatment**: Used to precipitate phosphate in sewage treatment.
3. **Agriculture**: Employed as a soil amendment to correct iron chlorosis in plants.
4. **Industry**: Used in the manufacturing of inks, wool dyeing, and as a mordant in textile dyeing.
5. **Laboratory Reagent**: Used in various analytical chemistry applications.

FERROUS GLUCONATE

Mol. Formula: $FeC_{12}H_{22}O_{14}.2H_2O$ **Mol. Weight:** 482.17

Physical Properties

1. **Appearance**: Ferrous gluconate is a yellowish to light brown powder.
2. **Solubility**: It is soluble in water and practically insoluble in alcohol.
3. **Melting Point**: It decomposes upon heating, so it does not have a well-defined melting point.
4. **Density**: The density is approximately 1.89 grams per cubic centimeter.
5. **Odor**: It is odorless.

Chemical Properties

1. **Chemical Formula**: $C_{12}H_{22}FeO_{14}$
2. **Molecular Weight**: The molecular weight of ferrous gluconate is approximately 446.14 grams per mole.
3. **Reactivity**: Ferrous gluconate can react with alkalis to form iron hydroxides and gluconic acid.

4. **Oxidation**: It is less prone to oxidation compared to ferrous sulphate, making it more stable in pharmaceutical formulations.

Preparation

Ferrous gluconate is typically prepared by reacting ferrous sulphate with gluconic acid:

$$FeSO_4 + 2C_6H_{11}O_7 \rightarrow Fe(C_6H_{11}O_7)_2 + H_2SO_4$$

Tests

1. **Iron Test**: Similar to ferrous sulphate, it forms a blue precipitate with potassium ferrocyanide.
2. **Gluconate Test**: The presence of gluconate can be confirmed by its reaction with specific enzymes or by chromatography.

Assay:

It is based on oxidation- reduction titration. Dissolve about 1.5 g of the dried sample, accurately weighed, in a mixture of 75 ml of water and 15 ml of dilute sulfuric acid in a 300-ml Erlenmeyer flask, and add 250 mg of zinc dust. Close the flask with a stopper containing a Bunsen valve, and allow to stand at room temperature for 20 min. Then filter through a Gooch crucible containing a glass fibre filter paper coated with a thin layer of zinc dust, and wash the crucible and contents with 10 ml of dilute sulfuric acid TS, followed by 10 ml of water. Add orthophenanthroline and titrate the filtrate in the suction flask immediately with 0.1 N ceric ammonium sulfate. Perform a blank determination, and make any necessary correction. Each ml of 0.1 N ceric ammonium sulfate is equivalent to 0.04461 g of $C_{12}H_{22}FeO_{14}$.

Uses

1. **Medicine**: Primarily used as an iron supplement for treating iron-deficiency anemia, especially where gastrointestinal tolerance is an issue.
2. **Food Additive**: Used to fortify foods with iron.
3. **Pharmaceuticals**: Included in various formulations due to its high bioavailability and better gastrointestinal tolerance compared to other iron salts.
4. **Veterinary Medicine**: Used to treat iron deficiency in animals.

CHAPTER – 17

POISON AND ANTIDOTES

Mr. Prabhanshu Vaishya

Assistant Professor, Rajiv Gandhi Institute of Pharmacy, Faculty of

Pharmaceutical Science & Technology, AKS University Satna, MP-India

ABSTRACT:

Poisons are substances that cause harm or death when introduced into the body in sufficient quantities. They can enter the body through ingestion, inhalation, injection, or absorption through the skin. Common poisons include chemicals like cyanide, heavy metals such as arsenic and lead, pesticides, household cleaners, and certain medications when taken inappropriately. The severity of poisoning depends on the dose, duration of exposure, and the individual's health condition. Symptoms of poisoning can range from mild, such as nausea and vomiting, to severe, including seizures, organ failure, and death. Antidotes are agents that counteract the effects of poisons. They work through various mechanisms: some neutralize the poison, others enhance its excretion, and some block its toxic effects on the body's cells and tissues. For example, activated charcoal can adsorb many toxins in the gastrointestinal tract, preventing their absorption. Naloxone is an antidote that reverses the effects of opioid overdose by binding to opioid receptors in the brain. Similarly, atropine is used to counteract poisoning by organophosphates, which are found in certain pesticides. Timely administration of the appropriate antidote is crucial for effective treatment of poisoning. In cases of unknown poisoning, supportive care, such as maintaining airway, breathing, and circulation, is vital while the specific poison is identified. Hospitals and poison control centers play essential roles in managing poisoning cases, offering expert advice and treatment protocols. Prevention remains the best strategy, involving safe storage of chemicals, proper use of medications, and awareness of potential hazards.

Education about common poisons and their antidotes can significantly reduce the risk of accidental poisoning. Public health initiatives often focus on informing the public about the dangers of certain substances and the importance of seeking immediate medical help in case of suspected poisoning. Despite advancements in medical treatments, the rapid response and administration of antidotes remain the cornerstone of poisoning management, emphasizing the need for readiness and quick action in emergency situations.

Introduction:

Poison: any substance that when introduce into or absorbed by a living organism causes illness or death. Anti-Dotes is an agent which counter act as poisons.

Classification of antidotes:

1. Physiological: Producing opposite effects to that poison e.g, Sodium nitrite in Cyanide poisoning Mechanical:- Prevent Absorption of Poison e.g, Activated Charcoal

2. Chemical: Change chemical nature of poison. e.g, Sodium thiosulphate in cyanide poisoning

SODIUM THIOSULPHATE

Mol. Formula: $Na_2S_2O_3.5H_2O$ **Mol. weight:** 248.17

Synonyms: Sodium hyposulphite; antichlor and Natrii thiosulfas.

Preparation:

1. Sodium thiosulfate is produced industrially from liquid waste products of sodium sulfide or during sulfur dye manufacture. An aqueous solution of sodium sulfite is heated with sulfur or by boiling aqueous sodium hydroxide and sulfur resulting into sodium thiosulfate on laboratory scale.

$$Na_2CO_3 + H_2O + 2SO_2 = 2NaHSO_3 + CO_2$$

$$2NaHSO_3 + Na_2CO_3 = 2Na_2S_2O_3 + H_2O + CO_2$$

2. It can be prepared by boiling sodium sulphite with sulphur.

$$Na_2SO_3 \;+\; S \;=\; Na_2S_2O_3$$

3. It is also prepared by reacting sodium hydroxide with sulphur.

$$6NaOH \;+\; 4S \;=\; Na_2S_2O_3 \;+\; 2Na_2S \;+\; 3H_2O$$

Physical Properties

1. **Appearance**: Sodium thiosulphate typically appears as colorless, crystalline solid or white powder.
2. **Solubility**: It is highly soluble in water, with a solubility of about 70 grams per 100 milliliters at 20 degrees Celsius. It is insoluble in ethanol.
3. **Melting Point**: The pentahydrate form melts at about 48 degrees Celsius.
4. **Density**: The density of the pentahydrate form is approximately 1.67 grams per cubic centimeter.
5. **Odor**: It is odorless.

Storage condition: It should be stored in air- tight container.

Tests

1. **Iodine Test**: Sodium thiosulphate solution decolorizes iodine solution, forming sodium iodide.
2. **Silver Nitrate Test**: When treated with silver nitrate, it forms a white precipitate of silver thiosulfate, which turns black upon exposure to light.

Chemical properties:

1. Sodium thiosulphate is decomposed by dilute acids, liberating sulphur di oxide with precipitation of sulphur.

$$Na_2S_2O_3 \;+\; 2HCl \;=\; 2NaCl \;+\; S \;+\; SO_2$$

2. The aqueous solution of Sodium thiosulphate decomposed slowly in cold water , but rapidly when heated.

$$4Na_2S_2O_3 \quad = \quad 3Na_2SO_4 + Na_2SO_4 + Na_2S_5$$

$$Na_2S_5 \quad = \quad Na_2S + 4S$$

3. Sodium thiosulphate react with barium chloride give precipitate of barium thiosulphate.

$$Na_2S_2O_3 + BaCl_2 \quad = \quad BaS_2O_3 + 2NaCl$$

4. It act as a reducing agents and reduces ferric chloride solution to form dark violet colour which quickly disappears.

$$3Na_2S_2O_3 + 2FeCl_3 \rightleftharpoons Fe_2(S_2O_3)_3 + 6NaCl$$

ASSAY:

The assay is based on Iodimetric titration. Dissolve about 0.5 g of the dried sample, accurately weighed, in 30 ml of water and titrate with 0.1 N iodine solution using starch solution as the indicator as the end point is obtained.
Each ml of 0.1 N iodine is equivalent to 0.02482 g of $Na_2S_2O_3.5H_2O$

$$2Na_2S_2O_3 + I_2 = Na_2S_4O_6 + 2NaI$$

Uses

1. **Photography**: Used as a fixer to dissolve unreacted silver halides from photographic films and papers.
2. **Medical Use**: Used in the treatment of cyanide poisoning and as an antifungal agent.
3. **Water Treatment**: Neutralizes chlorine in water treatment.
4. **Chemical Analysis**: Acts as a titrant in iodometric titrations.
5. **Gold Extraction**: Used in the leaching of gold from ores.
6. As mordant in dyeing and printing textiles and reducer in chrome dyeing and bacteriological water assessment.

SODIUM METABISULPHITE

Chemical formula: $Na_2S_2O_5$ **Mol. Wt.:** 190.10

Synonyms: Disodium pyrosulphite, sodium pyrosulphite

Preparation:

1. Sodium metabisulphite is prepared by saturating hot, concentrated sodium hydroxide solution with sulphur dioxide and allowing the salt to crystallize out. Sodium bisulphite, is first being unstable loses water and the solid metabisulphite separates out.

$$NaOH + SO_2 = NaHSO_3$$
$$2NaHSO_3 = Na_2S_2O_5 + H_2O$$

Physical Properties

1. **Appearance**: Sodium metabisulphite appears as a white or slightly yellow crystalline powder.
2. **Solubility**: It is soluble in water, with a solubility of about 65 grams per 100 milliliters at 20 degrees Celsius. It is insoluble in ethanol.
3. **Melting Point**: Decomposes upon heating before reaching a distinct melting point.
4. **Density**: The density is about 1.48 grams per cubic centimeter.
5. **Odor**: It has a strong sulfurous odor.

Chemical properties:

1. It is powerful reducing agent, when dissolved in water, it is immediately converted to bisulphite.

$$Na_2S_2O_5 + H_2O = 2NaHSO_3$$

2. Added acid in solution of sodium metabisulphite, sulphur dioxide gas is formed which is dissolved in solution a sulphurous acid.

$$Na_2S_2O_5 \xrightarrow{H^+} SO_2 \xrightarrow{H_2O} H_2SO_3$$

Tests

1. **Sulfur Dioxide Test**: When treated with acid, it releases sulfur dioxide gas, which can be detected by its pungent smell.
2. **Starch-Iodine Test**: It decolorizes iodine-starch complex, indicating its reducing nature.

Uses

1. **Food Industry**: Used as a preservative and antioxidant in food and beverages.
2. **Water Treatment**: Acts as a dechlorinating agent in water treatment.
3. **Photography**: Used in photographic developers.
4. **Chemical Industry**: Employed as a reducing agent and a sulfonating agent.
5. **Medical Use**: Used in certain pharmaceutical formulations as a preservative and antioxidant.

SODIUM NITRATE

Molecular formula: NaNO3   **Mol. Wt:** 69.0

Synonyms: nitrous acid sodium salt

Preparation:

1. It is prepared by strongly heating sodium nitrate.

$$2NaNO_3 \longrightarrow 2NaNO_2 + O_2$$

2. The gases formed during the catalytic oxidation of ammonium in sodium carbonate solution on absorption give sodium nitrate.

$$2Na_2CO_3 + 4NO + O_2 \longrightarrow 4NaNO_2 + 2CO_2$$

3. Sodium nitrate prepared by heating a mixture of sodium nitrate solution and quicklime and then passing air free SO2 through the solution.

$$NaNO_3 + CaO + SO_2 \longrightarrow CaSO_4 + NaNO_2$$

Physical Properties

1. **Appearance**: Sodium nitrate appears as a white, crystalline solid or powder.
2. **Solubility**: It is highly soluble in water, with a solubility of about 87.6 grams per 100 milliliters at 20 degrees Celsius.
3. **Melting Point**: The melting point is approximately 308 degrees Celsius.
4. **Density**: The density is about 2.26 grams per cubic centimeter.
5. **Odor**: It is odorless.

Storage: Stored in air tight container.

Chemical properties:

1. **Reactivity**: Sodium nitrate is a strong oxidizing agent and can react vigorously with reducing agents.
2. **Decomposition**: Upon heating, it decomposes to produce sodium nitrite and oxygen gas.
3. Its acts as a reducing as well as oxidizing agent. It is readily oxidized by $KClO_3$ or $KMnO_4$.

$$HClO_3 + 3HNO_2 \longrightarrow 3HNO_3 + KCl$$

$$2KMnO_4 + 5HNO_2 + 3H_2SO_4 \longrightarrow 2Mn_2SO_3 + 5HNO_3 + 3H_2O + K_2SO_4$$

4. Sulphuric acid reacts with sodium nitrite solution forming nitrous oxide.

$$2NaNO_2 + H_2SO_4 \longrightarrow Na_2SO_3 + 2HNO_2$$
$$\downarrow$$
$$H_2O + NO + HNO_3$$

5. Sodium nitrite with aniline hydrochloride at 40C, nitrous acid forms diazonium chloride.

$$C_6H_5NH_2.HCl + HNO_2 \longrightarrow C_6H_5N_2Cl + 2H_2O$$

Tests

1. **Flame Test**: Sodium nitrate imparts a yellow color to the flame due to the sodium ion.
2. **Reaction with Ferrous Sulfate**: When mixed with ferrous sulfate and sulfuric acid, it forms a brown ring at the interface, indicating the presence of nitrates.

Uses

1. **Fertilizer**: Used as a nitrogen source in fertilizers.
2. **Food Industry**: Acts as a preservative and color fixative in cured meats.
3. **Explosives**: Used in the manufacture of explosives and pyrotechnics.
4. **Chemical Industry**: Employed in the production of nitric acid and sodium nitrite.
5. **Heat Transfer**: Used in heat transfer and thermal storage systems.

CHAPTER – 18

ASTRINGENTS

Mr. Santosh Kumar

Assistant Professor, Rajiv Gandhi Institute of Pharmacy, Faculty of Pharmaceutical Science & Technology, AKS University Satna, MP-India

ABSTRACT:

Astringents are chemical agents that cause the contraction of body tissues, primarily used to reduce bleeding from minor abrasions and to shrink tissues. They work by precipitating proteins on the surface of cells, forming a protective barrier and reducing irritation and inflammation. Commonly found in skin care products, astringents help to cleanse the skin, tighten pores, and reduce oiliness, making them beneficial for individuals with oily or acne-prone skin. Traditional astringents include witch hazel, alum, and tannic acid, while modern formulations often contain alcohol or other synthetic compounds. In addition to their dermatological uses, astringents are utilized in various medical and dental applications. For instance, they are employed in mouthwashes to reduce oral inflammation and in throat lozenges to soothe sore throats. In wound care, astringents like silver nitrate are used to control minor bleeding and promote healing. The use of astringents in eye drops helps to reduce redness and discomfort by constricting blood vessels. While generally safe for topical use, astringents should be used with caution, as overuse can lead to excessive dryness, irritation, and skin sensitivity. It is essential to choose astringents appropriate for one's skin type and to follow usage instructions to avoid adverse effects. In therapeutic settings, the concentration and formulation of astringents are carefully controlled to maximize efficacy and minimize potential side effects. The effectiveness of astringents in various applications underscores their versatility and importance in personal care and medical treatments. Continued research and development aim to enhance their formulations, making them more effective and suitable for a broader range of uses. Whether in everyday skincare routines or specialized medical treatments, astringents remain valuable tools for managing skin health and treating minor ailments.

Introduction:

It is a chemical that shrinks or constricts body tissues.

The word "astringents" derives from Latin adstringere , meaning to " to bind fast". Astringents are locally applied protein precipitants which have a low cell permeability so that the limited essentially to the cell surface and the interstitial spaces.

Nearly all astringents coagulate albumin, tone up relaxed or debilitated condition of muscular fiber, contract both artioles and capillaries, restrain peristailsis, contract gland duct and repress excessive secretions.

ZINC SULPHATE

Mol. Formula: $ZnSO_4.7H_2O$ **Mol. Wt.:** 287.54

Synonym: White vitriol

Physical Properties:

- **Appearance**: White crystalline powder or colorless crystals.
- **Molecular Weight**: 161.47 g/mol (heptahydrate), 179.45 g/mol (monohydrate).
- **Solubility**: Highly soluble in water (57.7 g/100 mL at 20 °C); insoluble in alcohol.
- **Density**: 3.54 g/cm³ (anhydrous), 1.97 g/cm³ (heptahydrate).
- **Melting Point**: Decomposes at 680 °C.
- **Odor and Taste**: Odorless with an astringent taste.

Preparation: Zinc sulphate can be prepared by:

1. **Direct Synthesis:**
   - Reacting zinc metal or zinc oxide with sulfuric acid:
     $$Zn+H_2SO_4 \rightarrow ZnSO_4+H_2 \quad ZnO+H_2SO4 \rightarrow ZnSO_4+H_2O$$

- o $ZnO + H_2SO_4 \rightarrow ZnSO_4 + H_2O$

2. **By-Product Recovery**:

   - o As a by-product in the production of other zinc compounds.

Chemical Properties:

- **Chemical Formula**: $ZnSO_4$.

- **Reactivity**: Reacts with bases to form zinc hydroxide. Hydrates form dissolve in water to produce acidic solutions.

- **Stability**: Stable under normal conditions. Loses water of crystallization upon heating.

Storage:

- **Conditions**: Store in a cool, dry place in tightly closed containers.

- **Precautions**: Protect from moisture and incompatible substances like strong acids and bases.

Uses:

1. **Medical**:

   - o **Nutritional Supplement**: Used to treat zinc deficiency.

   - o **Astringent**: Used in lotions and ointments for its astringent properties.

2. **Agriculture**:

   - o **Fertilizer**: Provides zinc, an essential micronutrient for plant growth.

3. **Industrial**:

   - o **Electroplating**: Used in zinc plating to prevent corrosion.

4. **Laboratory**:

   - o **Analytical Reagent**: Used in various chemical analyses.

Official Preparation: Zinc Sulphate Tablets USP

- **Formulation**: Typically available as 220 mg tablets of zinc sulphate monohydrate.

- **Usage**: Prescribed for the treatment of zinc deficiency and related conditions.
- **Dosage**: Varies depending on the condition and patient needs, commonly 1-2 tablets daily.
- **Administration**: Taken orally with water, preferably with food to reduce gastrointestinal irritation.

Storage of Official Preparations:

- **Conditions**: Store at room temperature in a tightly closed container.
- **Precautions**: Keep out of reach of children and follow expiration dates.

POTASH ALUM

Mol. Formula: $KAl(SO_4)_2.12H_2O$ **Mol. Wt.:** 474.33

Synonyms: Aluminium potassium sulphate

Physical Properties:

- **Appearance**: Colorless to white crystalline solid.
- **Molecular Weight**: 474.39 g/mol.
- **Solubility**: Soluble in water (14.00 g/100 mL at 20 °C); insoluble in alcohol.
- **Density**: 1.725 g/cm³.
- **Melting Point**: 92.5 °C (loses water and decomposes).
- **Odor and Taste**: Odorless with a sweetish, astringent taste.

Preparation: Potash alum can be prepared by:

1. **Natural Sources**:
   - Mined from natural mineral deposits.
2. **Synthetic Preparation**:
   - Mixing potassium sulfate (K_2SO_4) and aluminum sulfate ($Al_2(SO_4)_3$) in water and crystallizing:

     $$K_2SO_4 + Al_2(SO_4)_3 + 24H_2O \rightarrow 2KAl(SO_4)2 \cdot 12H2O$$

     $$K_2SO_4 + Al_2(SO_4)_3 + 24H_2O \rightarrow 2KAl(SO_4)_2 \cdot 12H_2O$$

Chemical Properties:

- **Chemical Formula**: $KAl(SO_4)_2 \cdot 12H_2O$.
- **Reactivity**: Reacts with bases to form aluminum hydroxide. Dissolves in water to form acidic solutions.
- **Stability**: Stable under normal conditions. Loses water of crystallization upon heating.

Storage:

- **Conditions**: Store in a cool, dry place in tightly closed containers.
- **Precautions**: Protect from moisture and contaminants.

Uses:

1. **Medical**:
   - **Astringent**: Used in styptic pencils to stop bleeding from minor cuts.
   - **Antiseptic**: Used in some topical formulations.
2. **Water Treatment**:
   - **Flocculant**: Used to clarify water by causing impurities to coagulate and settle.
3. **Cosmetics**:
   - **Deodorant**: Used in natural deodorants for its antimicrobial properties.
4. **Industrial**:
   - **Paper Manufacturing**: Used in the sizing of paper to improve its quality.

Official Preparation: Potash Alum Topical Solution USP

- **Formulation**: Typically available as a 5% to 10% aqueous solution.
- **Usage**: Used as an astringent and antiseptic in various topical applications.
- **Dosage**: Applied directly to the affected area as needed.
- **Administration**: For external use only.

Storage of Official Preparations:

- **Conditions**: Store at room temperature in a tightly closed container.

- **Precautions**: Keep out of reach of children and avoid contact with eyes. Follow expiration dates and usage instructions.

CHAPTER – 19

RADIOPHARMACEUTICALS – I

Mr. Ram Prasad Sahu

Assistant Professor, Rajiv Gandhi Institute of Pharmacy, Faculty of

Pharmaceutical Science & Technology, AKS University Satna, MP-India

----

ABSTACT:

Radiopharmaceuticals are specialized medicinal formulations containing radioisotopes used in the diagnosis and treatment of various diseases. These compounds emit radiation that can be detected by imaging devices such as PET (Positron Emission Tomography) and SPECT (Single Photon Emission Computed Tomography), allowing for the visualization of physiological processes at the molecular level. This capability makes radiopharmaceuticals indispensable in detecting and monitoring conditions like cancer, cardiovascular diseases, and neurological disorders. Therapeutically, radiopharmaceuticals can deliver targeted radiation to diseased tissues, such as in the treatment of thyroid cancer with iodine-131 or bone pain palliation in metastatic cancer with strontium-89. The preparation of radiopharmaceuticals involves stringent protocols to ensure purity, sterility, and accurate dosage, given their radioactive nature and the need for patient safety. Their administration requires specialized facilities and trained personnel to handle the radioactive materials and to minimize radiation exposure. The development and application of radiopharmaceuticals are regulated by health authorities to ensure compliance with safety standards. Advances in radiopharmaceutical research continue to expand their diagnostic and therapeutic applications, improving the precision and efficacy of medical treatments.Proper storage and handling are critical to maintain the stability and effectiveness of radiopharmaceuticals. They must be stored in shielded, secure environments to protect both healthcare workers and the environment from radiation exposure. As the field of nuclear medicine evolves, the integration of radiopharmaceuticals with other diagnostic and therapeutic modalities is expected to enhance personalized medicine, providing tailored treatments based on the specific molecular characteristics of a patient's condition. This approach promises to improve outcomes and reduce side effects, marking a significant advancement in medical science.

Introduction:

Radiopharmaceuticals: Compounds or substances which emit radiations and which are used in pharmacy. Similar words are used for these substances like Radio-Isotopes, Radio nuclide and radioisotopes.

Radioactivity: The process of emitting radiations by unstable isotopes is known as radioactivity and this type of isotopes are known as radioactive isotopes.

Radio Isotopes: These are the unstable isotopes which emits radiations.

Isotopes: Atoms of an element which have the same atomic number but which have different mass numbers are called as isotopes.

Half-life of radio isotopes: It is defined as the time required for a radioactive isotope to decay to one half of it's original value at any given point of time.

Atomic No.: It is equal to no. of protons present in the nucleus of its atom.

Mass No.: It is the sum of the no. of protons & the no. of neutrons.

Unit of radiations:

The fundamental units of radioactivity are:

Curie (Ci), Millicurie (mCi), Microcurie, Bequerel (Bq), Electron volt (eV), Roentagen (R), Rad.

Curie: It is defined as the quantity of the radioactive substance undergoing $3.7 \times 10^{10 \text{ disintegrations}}$ per second.

1 Ci = 3.7×10^{10} Bq.

Becquerel: It is the SI unit of activity defined as 1 transformation per second.

1 Bq = 2.7×10^{-11} Ci.

1 Electron volt (eV) = 1.6×10^{-19} J.

1 Rad $= 10^{-2}$ J Kg^{-1},

1 Roentgen $= 2.58 \times 10^{-4}$ CKg^{-1}

Half-life of nuclides:

Definition: It is defined as the time required for a radioactive isotope to decay one half of it's original value at any given point of time.

Example: we have 64 micro curies of radioactivity in a given sample of ferric citrate solution on date 1.3.2006 to 3.5.2006.

- 64 mCi (After 1st t$^{1/2}$ life period i.e. after 45 days)
- 32 mCi (After the 2nd t$^{1/2}$)
- 16 mCi (After the 3rd t$^{1/2}$)

- 8 mCi (After the 4th t$^{1/2}$) 4

Types of radiation:

S. No	Alfa particles/ rays	Beta particle/ rays	Gamma Particles/ rays
1.	Positive charge.	Negative charge.	Neutral
2.	High Ionizing power.	Less than alpha particles.	Low ionizing power.
3.	Lowest penetrating power	100 times more penetration than alpha particles.	10,000 times more than Beta particles.
4.	Can stopped by even a piece of thin paper	Blocked aluminium plate	It can pass block, aluminium plate also.
5.	Heavy in nature.	Negligible mass.	Light in weight.
6.	Used in medicines for diagnosis & treatment. Ex.Helium	Used in medicines for diagnosis & treatment. EX-I 131	Used in medicines for diagnosis & treatment.

Measurement of radioactivity:

Two main detectors used for radiation detection and measurements are:

A) Gas Filled Detectors:

    1) Ionization Chambers.

    2) Proportional Counters.

    3) Geiger-Muller (G.M. Counter).

B) Scintillation Detectors:

  1) Inorganic scintillators.

  2) Organic scintillators.

  3) Semiconductor detectors.

  4) Photographic emulsions.

  5) Crenekor detectors.

  6) Thermo luminescence dosimeters.

  7) Tract-etch detectors.

Geiger-Muller Counter:

Principle

The Geiger-Muller (GM) counter operates on the principle of gas ionization. When ionizing radiation passes through the inert gas-filled tube of the counter, it ionizes the gas molecules, producing ions and free electrons. These charged particles are then attracted to the electrodes, creating an electrical pulse that is counted and measured. The magnitude of the pulse is independent of the energy of the ionizing particle, making the GM counter a reliable detector for measuring radiation levels.

Construction

1. **Tube**: The GM tube is typically a cylindrical glass or metal tube filled with an inert gas such as helium, neon, or argon at low pressure. Sometimes a halogen or organic vapor is added as a quenching agent.

2. **Electrodes**: Inside the tube, there is a central wire (anode) and a conductive outer shell (cathode). The anode is connected to a high-voltage power supply.

3. **Window**: In some GM counters, particularly those designed to detect alpha and beta particles, there is a thin window made of mica or another low-density material to allow the particles to enter the tube.

4. **Quenching Agent**: The quenching agent, either in the form of a gas or a chemical coating on the anode, stops the discharge by absorbing the excess energy from the ionized gas molecules.

Working

1. **Ionization**: When ionizing radiation (such as alpha particles, beta particles, or gamma rays) enters the Geiger-Muller tube, it ionizes the gas inside.

2. **Electron Avalanche**: The initial ionization event releases electrons, which are accelerated towards the positively charged anode by the high voltage applied across the electrodes. As these electrons collide with gas molecules, they create more ionizations, resulting in an avalanche of electrons.

3. **Pulse Formation**: The avalanche of electrons creates a measurable electrical pulse. This pulse is picked up by the anode and sent to an external counting device.

4. **Quenching**: To prevent continuous discharge (which would cause the counter to fail to detect individual radiation events), a quenching gas or an electrical mechanism halts the ionization process, allowing the counter to reset for the next detection event.

5. **Educational Tools**: GM counters are used in educational settings to demonstrate the principles of radiation detection and nuclear physics to students.

6. **Industrial Applications**: In industries such as oil and gas, GM counters are used to detect naturally occurring radioactive materials (NORM) and ensure compliance with safety regulations.

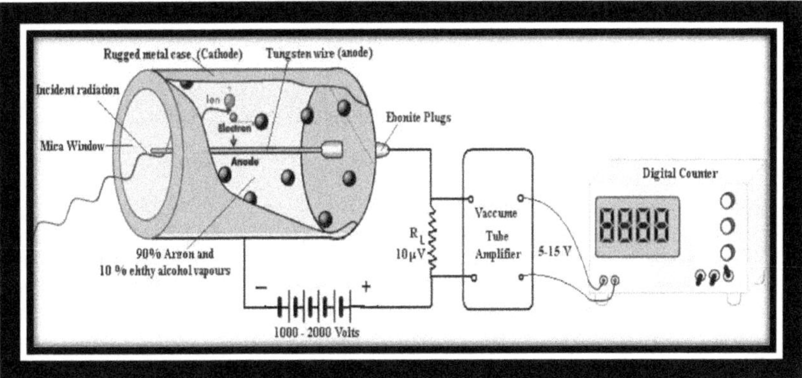

Procedure of Using a Geiger-Muller Counter

Preparation

1. **Inspection**: Inspect the Geiger-Muller (GM) counter for any physical damage. Ensure that the probe, cables, and connectors are intact.
2. **Battery Check**: If the device is battery-operated, check the battery level and replace or recharge the batteries if necessary.
3. **Calibration**: Verify that the GM counter is properly calibrated. Calibration should be performed according to the manufacturer's instructions or relevant standards, typically using a known radiation source.

Operation

1. **Power On**: Turn on the GM counter using the power switch. Allow it to warm up if required, as specified by the manufacturer.

2. **Select Mode**: Set the GM counter to the desired measurement mode (e.g., counts per minute (CPM), dose rate in microsieverts per hour (μSv/h), etc.).

3. **Background Measurement**: Before taking any specific readings, measure the background radiation level. Hold the probe away from any known radiation sources and record the background count. This will help in distinguishing between normal background radiation and elevated levels due to specific sources.

4. **Positioning the Probe**: Hold the probe close to the surface or area being tested. Ensure that the window of the probe faces the potential radiation source for optimal detection. For alpha or beta particles, the probe may need to be positioned very close to or in direct contact with the source due to their limited range in air.

5. **Taking Readings**: Allow the GM counter to collect data for a sufficient period to get a stable reading. This might be a few seconds to a few minutes, depending on the radiation level and desired accuracy. The device will typically produce audible clicks or visual indicators for each detection event.

6. **Recording Data**: Record the readings displayed on the GM counter. If the device provides multiple units of measurement, ensure that you note the correct unit (e.g., CPM, μSv/h).

7. **Comparison with Background**: Subtract the background radiation level from the measured level to determine the net radiation level from the source.

Post-Operation

1. **Turn Off**: After completing the measurements, turn off the GM counter to conserve battery life.

2. **Data Logging**: If the GM counter has data logging capabilities, save the data for future reference or analysis.

3. **Decontamination**: If the probe has been in contact with radioactive materials, decontaminate it according to safety protocols to avoid spreading contamination.

4. **Storage**: Store the GM counter in a safe, dry place, away from sources of radiation and extreme temperatures.

Safety Considerations

1. **Personal Protection**: Wear appropriate personal protective equipment (PPE) such as gloves and lab coats when handling radioactive materials.

2. **Avoid Contamination**: Ensure that the GM counter and its probe do not become contaminated with radioactive materials. Use protective coverings if necessary.

3. **Follow Regulations**: Adhere to all relevant safety regulations and guidelines for radiation protection and use of radiation detection equipment.

4. **Radiation Sources**: Handle radiation sources with care and follow proper protocols to prevent unnecessary exposure.

Troubleshooting

1. **Erratic Readings**: If the readings are erratic or unusually high, check for potential sources of interference, such as electronic devices or other radiation sources.

2. **Low Battery**: Replace or recharge the battery if the device shows low battery warnings.

3. **Calibration**: If the readings appear inaccurate, recalibrate the GM counter according to the manufacturer's instructions or contact a service provider for professional calibration.

Applications

1. **Radiation Monitoring**: GM counters are widely used in health physics and radiological protection to monitor environmental radiation levels and ensure safety in workplaces such as nuclear power plants, medical facilities, and research laboratories.

2. **Personal Dosimeters**: Portable GM counters are used by individuals working in environments where radiation exposure is possible, providing real-time monitoring of radiation levels.

3. **Survey Instruments**: GM counters are employed in radiation surveys to detect and measure radioactive contamination in various settings, including environmental assessments and decontamination efforts.

Scintillation Counters (For gamma counting):

Principle of Scintillation Counters

Scintillation counters detect and measure ionizing radiation by utilizing the scintillation process, where certain materials emit light (scintillate) when they absorb ionizing radiation. This emitted light is then converted into an electrical signal, which can be measured and analyzed.

Construction of Scintillation Counters

1. **Scintillator Material**: This is the core component where the scintillation occurs. It can be a crystal (like sodium iodide doped with thallium, NaI(Tl)), a liquid, or a plastic scintillator.

2. **Photomultiplier Tube (PMT)**: Attached to the scintillator, the PMT converts the light photons into an electrical signal. It amplifies this signal through multiple stages.

3. **High Voltage Power Supply**: Provides the necessary voltage to the PMT for operation.

4. **Pulse Processing Electronics**: This includes amplifiers, discriminators, and counters to process and count the pulses generated by the PMT.

5. **Shielding**: Often, scintillation counters are shielded with materials like lead to protect from background radiation and improve measurement accuracy.

Working of Scintillation Counters

1. **Ionizing Radiation Interaction**: When gamma rays (or other ionizing radiation) interact with the scintillator material, they cause the material to emit light photons.

2. **Light Photon Collection**: These light photons are collected and directed towards the PMT.

3. **Photon to Electron Conversion**: The PMT's photocathode converts the light photons into electrons through the photoelectric effect.

4. **Electron Multiplication**: The initial electrons are multiplied through a series of dynodes in the PMT, producing a larger number of electrons and thus amplifying the signal.

5. **Signal Processing**: The amplified electrical signal is processed by the pulse processing electronics, which count the pulses and provide a measurement of the radiation intensity.

Applications of Scintillation Counters

1. **Medical Imaging**: Used in gamma cameras for nuclear medicine imaging, including PET (Positron Emission Tomography) and SPECT (Single Photon Emission Computed Tomography).

2. **Environmental Monitoring**: Employed in detecting and measuring environmental radiation levels, including contamination and background radiation.

3. **Nuclear Physics Research**: Utilized in experiments to detect and measure radiation from nuclear reactions.

4. **Security and Defense**: Used in radiation detection equipment for security screening and defense applications to detect illicit radioactive materials.

5. **Industrial Applications**: Applied in non-destructive testing, oil well logging, and radiography for material analysis and quality control.

Advantages of Scintillation Counting:

1. The rapidity of fluorescence decay (10-9s), which, when compared to dead time in a Geiger-Muller tube (10-4s), means much higher count rates is possible.

2. The ability to accommodate samples of any type, including liquids, solids, suspensions and gels.

3. The general ease of sample preparation.

4. The ability to count separately different isotopes in the same sample, which means dual labelling experiments, can be carried out.

5. Scintillation counters are highly automated, hundreds of samples can be counted automatically and built-in computer facilities carry out many forms of data analysis, such as efficiency correction, graph plotting, radioimmunoassay calculations, etc.

Disadvantages of Scintillation Counting:

1. The cost per sample of scintillation counting is not insignificant

2. Low cost photomultipliers, however, have been designed to provide greater temperature systems.

CHAPTER – 20

RADIOPHARMACEUTICALS

Mr. Sachin Singh

Assistant Professor, Rajiv Gandhi Institute of Pharmacy, Faculty of

Pharmaceutical Science & Technology, AKS University Satna, MP-India

ABSTACT:

Radiopharmaceuticals, specifically radio-opaque contrast media, play a crucial role in diagnostic imaging by enhancing the visibility of internal structures in radiographic procedures. These substances are administered to patients to increase the contrast of images obtained from X-rays, computed tomography (CT) scans, and other imaging modalities. Radio-opaque contrast media are typically composed of iodine or barium compounds due to their high atomic numbers, which effectively absorb X-rays and improve image clarity. Iodine-based contrast agents are commonly used for vascular and soft tissue imaging, while barium sulphate suspensions are preferred for gastrointestinal tract examinations.The administration of these contrast agents allows for the detailed visualization of blood vessels, organs, and other tissues, aiding in the accurate diagnosis and management of various medical conditions such as tumors, blockages, and abnormalities in organ structure and function. Despite their widespread use, it is essential to consider potential adverse reactions, such as allergic responses or nephrotoxicity, particularly in patients with pre-existing conditions. Advances in contrast media technology continue to focus on enhancing safety profiles, reducing side effects, and improving the efficacy of these agents in clinical practice.

Applications of radiopharmaceuticals in pharmacy:

Radiopharmaceuticals are used in various branches like:

1. Diagnostic applications.

2. Radiotherapy.

3. Sterilization.

4. For Research.

5. Analytical Applications.

1. **Diagnostic applications:**

   a. Phosphorus 32: Used for diagnosis of cancer.

   b. Chromium51: Used for diagnosis of red cell survival & volume: it is also used to estimate GI blood losses through stool or urine.

   c. Cobalt 57, 58: Used for measurement of absorption of vit.-B_{12}. Diagnosis of Pernicious anemia.

   d. Iodine-131: Determination of Thyroid function.

   e. Labelled cyanocobalamin finds use for measuring the glomerular filtration rate.

   f. Ferric citrate injection finds use for the diagnosis of haematological disorders.

   g. Colloidal gold injection is used diagnostically to study blood circulation in liver.

   h. Sodium iodide injection finds use in diagnosis of proper functioning of thyroid gland.

   i. Sodium iodohippurate injection finds use in the study of renal function.

   j. Sodium rose Bengal injection finds use as diagnostic agent to test liver function.

2. **Radiotherapy**: Some radioisotopes are having ability to destroy the disease without destroying healthy tissues.

a) Iodine 131: Used in the treatment of hyperthyroidism. It also used in the treatment of thyroid cancer.

b) Cobalt 60: Used in treatment of cancer involving cervix, vagina, uterus, bladder, mouth, tongue and lips.

c) Phosphorus 32: Used in treatment of various types of cancer in polycythaemia (erythrocytosis) & Leukemia.

d) Gold1 94 used as antineoplasatic.

e) Holmium 66 (26 h) being developed for diagnosis and treatment of liver tumours.

f) Iodine-125 (60 d) used in cancer brachytherapy (prostate and brain).

g) Iodine 123 used as antineoplastic

3. **Sterilization:**

- Excellent use is being made of the radiation constantly available from some strong radiation source for sterilizing pharmaceuticals in their final packed containers and surgical instruments in hospitals

- Used for sterilization of thermolabile drugs like Hormones, Vitamins, Antibiotics, Surgical dressings, Disposable syringes.

- Examples: Cobalt 60: Used for the sterilization of disposable syringes,   catheters and surgical dressings

4. **Research application:** Used in bio chemical reactions, may be used for detection of mechanism of reactions. Examples: Iodine 131, Sodium 24 and Phosphorus 32.

5. **Analytical application:** Plays major role   when dealing with dilute solutions

Handling of radiopharmaceuticals:

Handling radiopharmaceuticals requires stringent protocols to ensure safety for both healthcare personnel and patients, given their radioactive nature. These substances are used in various diagnostic and therapeutic procedures, and proper handling minimizes radiation exposure and contamination risks.

Safety Protocols:

1. **Training and Certification**:
   - Personnel handling radiopharmaceuticals must receive specialized training in radiation safety, handling techniques, and emergency procedures.
   - Certification by relevant authorities ensures that handlers are knowledgeable about the safe use of radioactive materials.

2. **Facility Requirements**:
   - Radiopharmaceuticals should be prepared and stored in designated areas that meet regulatory standards for radiation safety.
   - These areas must have appropriate shielding, ventilation, and monitoring equipment to detect radiation levels.

3. **Personal Protective Equipment (PPE)**:
   - Handlers must wear appropriate PPE, including lead aprons, gloves, and eye protection, to reduce exposure.
   - Use of dosimeters to monitor individual radiation exposure is essential.

4. **Preparation and Administration**:
   - Use lead-shielded syringes and vials during preparation and administration to minimize radiation exposure.
   - Follow strict aseptic techniques to prevent contamination and ensure patient safety.
   - Verify the correct radiopharmaceutical and dosage before administration.

5. **Storage and Transportation**:
   - Store radiopharmaceuticals in lead-lined containers and secure, designated storage areas.

o Transport them in compliance with regulatory guidelines, using shielded containers to protect handlers and the environment.

6. **Waste Management**:

   o Dispose of radioactive waste following strict protocols to prevent environmental contamination.

   o Use designated disposal containers for radioactive waste and follow regulatory guidelines for storage and disposal.

7. **Emergency Procedures**:

   o Have clear protocols for managing spills, contamination, or accidental exposure.

   o Immediate steps should include evacuating the area, containing the spill, and notifying radiation safety officers.

8. **Documentation and Record-Keeping**:

   o Maintain accurate records of radiopharmaceutical usage, including amounts received, used, and disposed of.

   o Document radiation exposure levels for personnel and ensure compliance with regulatory limits.

9. **Patient Safety**:

   o Provide patients with clear instructions regarding post-procedure safety, such as avoiding close contact with others for a specified period.

   o Monitor patients for adverse reactions and provide appropriate follow-up care.

10. **Regulatory Compliance**:

   o Adhere to all local, national, and international regulations regarding the use of radiopharmaceuticals.

   o Regular audits and inspections ensure compliance with safety standards and protocols.

Radioactive Liquids:

- Working area should not get contaminated with radioactive material.
- If radioactive liquid is to be handled, it must be carried in trays with absorbent tissue paper, so that any spillage will get absorbed by the paper.
- Rubber gloves have to be used when working with radioactive liquids.
- Pipettes operated by mouth should never be used.
- Waste of radioactive material has to be stored till its activity becomes low and then only it should be disposed.

Storage of radiopharmaceuticals:

Proper storage of radiopharmaceuticals is critical to ensure their safety, efficacy, and compliance with regulatory standards. Here are the key guidelines and considerations for the storage of radiopharmaceuticals:

Storage Guidelines

1. **Designated Storage Areas**:
   - Radiopharmaceuticals must be stored in designated areas that are specifically designed and constructed to handle radioactive materials.
   - These areas should be clearly marked with radiation hazard signs to prevent unauthorized access.

2. **Shielding**:
   - Storage areas should have adequate shielding to minimize radiation exposure to personnel and the environment. This often involves using lead-lined cabinets or containers.
   - The level of shielding required depends on the type and activity level of the radiopharmaceuticals being stored.

3. **Temperature Control**:
   - o Many radiopharmaceuticals require specific temperature conditions to maintain their stability and efficacy. This may include refrigeration or room temperature storage.
   - o Storage areas should be equipped with temperature monitoring devices to ensure consistent and appropriate environmental conditions.
4. **Security**:
   - o Access to storage areas should be restricted to authorized personnel only. Secure locks, surveillance systems, and access control measures should be in place.
   - o Inventory records should be maintained to track the receipt, usage, and disposal of radiopharmaceuticals.
5. **Ventilation**:
   - o Adequate ventilation is necessary to prevent the buildup of radioactive gases and to control the spread of contamination in the event of a spill.
   - o Fume hoods or specialized ventilation systems may be required, especially for volatile radiopharmaceuticals.
6. **Segregation**:
   - o Different types of radiopharmaceuticals should be stored separately to prevent cross-contamination and to facilitate proper handling.
   - o Short-lived isotopes should be segregated from long-lived isotopes, and liquids should be stored separately from solids.
7. **Spill Containment**:
   - o Storage areas should be equipped with spill containment kits and materials to quickly manage and mitigate any accidental releases.
   - o Floors and surfaces should be non-porous and easy to decontaminate.

Regulatory Compliance

1. **Local and National Regulations**:
   - Follow all local, national, and international regulations regarding the storage of radioactive materials. This includes guidelines from regulatory bodies such as the Nuclear Regulatory Commission (NRC) in the United States or equivalent authorities in other countries.
   - Regular audits and inspections should be conducted to ensure compliance with these regulations.

2. **Record-Keeping**:
   - Maintain detailed records of all radiopharmaceuticals in storage, including information on their activity levels, storage conditions, and expiration dates.
   - Document any incidents, such as spills or breaches in storage protocol, and the corrective actions taken.

3. **Training**:
   - Ensure that all personnel involved in the handling and storage of radiopharmaceuticals are adequately trained in radiation safety, emergency procedures, and proper storage techniques.
   - Ongoing training and refresher courses should be provided to keep personnel up-to-date with current best practices and regulatory changes.

Best Practices

1. **Regular Inspections**:
   - Conduct regular inspections of storage areas to check for compliance with safety protocols and to identify any potential issues.
   - Ensure that shielding, temperature controls, and security measures are functioning correctly.

2. **Inventory Management**:
   - Implement a robust inventory management system to track the movement of radiopharmaceuticals and to prevent stockpiling of expired or unused materials.
   - Use a first-in, first-out (FIFO) system to ensure that older materials are used before newer ones.
3. **Emergency Preparedness**:
   - Develop and regularly update emergency response plans for incidents involving radiopharmaceuticals, including spills, fires, and security breaches.
   - Conduct periodic drills to ensure that personnel are familiar with emergency procedures and can respond effectively in the event of an incident.

RADIO-OPAQUE CONTRAST MEDIA

1. Radio-opaque substances are those compounds (both inorganic and organic) which are having the property of casting a shadow on X-ray films.
2. These compounds have the ability to stop the passage of X-rays and appear opaque on X-ray examination.

BARIUM SULPHATE

Mol. Formula: $BaSO_4$ **Mol. Wt.:** 233.39

Physical Properties:

- **Appearance**: White crystalline powder or heavy, white, odorless crystals.
- **Molecular Weight**: 233.39 g/mol.
- **Melting Point**: 1,580 °C.
- **Solubility**: Insoluble in water and organic solvents; soluble in concentrated sulfuric acid.

- **Density**: 4.5 g/cm³.
- **Odor and Taste**: Odorless and tasteless.

Preparation: Barium sulphate can be prepared by the following methods:

1. **From Barite Ore**:
   - Barium sulphate is naturally found as the mineral barite (also known as baryte). It is mined and then purified for various uses.
2. It is also prepared by the action of dilute H_2SO_4 on BaS

$$BaS + H_2SO_4 \ = \ BaSO_4 + H_2S$$

3. **Precipitation Method**:
   - By reacting barium chloride ($BaCl_2$) with sodium sulphate (Na_2SO_4) in an aqueous solution, barium sulphate precipitates out.

     $BaCl_2 + Na_2SO_4 \rightarrow BaSO_4 + 2NaCl$
   - The precipitate is filtered, washed, and dried to obtain pure barium sulphate.
4. For pharmaceutical purposes, Barium sulphate is prepared by treating an aqueous solution containing Barium ions with a solution containing sulphate ions.

$$Ba(OH)_2 + H_2SO_4 = BaSO_4 + 2H_2O$$
$$BaCl_2 + H_2SO_4 = BaSO_4 + 2HCl$$

Chemical Properties:

- **Chemical Formula**: $BaSO_4$.
- **Reactivity**: Chemically inert under normal conditions.
- **Stability**: Stable; does not decompose under normal conditions. Resistant to acids and bases, except concentrated sulfuric acid.

Storage:

- **Conditions**: Store in a cool, dry place in tightly closed containers.
- **Precautions**: Protect from moisture and contamination. Ensure proper labeling and handling to prevent inhalation of dust.

Uses:

1. **Medical**:
   - **Radiology**: Used as a contrast agent in X-ray imaging and other radiographic procedures to visualize the gastrointestinal tract.
2. **Industrial**:
   - **Paints and Coatings**: Used as a white pigment and filler to improve the quality and durability of paints and coatings.
   - **Plastics**: Acts as a filler to improve the density and properties of plastic products.
   - **Rubber**: Used as a filler and to improve the properties of rubber compounds.
3. **Oil and Gas**:
   - **Drilling Fluids**: Added to drilling fluids to increase the density and control the pressure in oil and gas wells.

Official Preparation: Barium Sulphate Suspension USP

1. **Formulation**: An aqueous suspension of barium sulphate, typically at concentrations ranging from 60% to 100% w/v, depending on the specific use.
2. **Usage**: Used as a contrast agent in radiographic procedures to enhance the visibility of the gastrointestinal tract.
3. **Dosage**: The dosage depends on the type of imaging study and the area of the gastrointestinal tract being examined. Typically administered orally or rectally under medical supervision.

4. **Administration**: For oral or rectal use under the direction of a healthcare provider. Patients may be instructed to fast or follow specific dietary restrictions prior to the procedure.

Storage of Official Preparations:

1. **Conditions**: Store at room temperature in a tightly closed container.
2. **Precautions**: Shake well before use to ensure a uniform suspension. Keep out of reach of children and follow specific storage instructions provided by the manufacturer.

Safety Information:

1. **Side Effects**: Generally well-tolerated. Possible side effects include nausea, vomiting, constipation, or abdominal discomfort. Rarely, allergic reactions may occur.
2. **Contraindications**: Not recommended for individuals with known hypersensitivity to barium sulphate or with gastrointestinal perforation or obstruction.
3. **Interactions**: Inform healthcare providers of all medications and supplements being taken to avoid potential interactions.